THE BEST IS
YET TO BE

THE BEST IS YET TO BE

RENEWING AMERICAN JUDAISM

Rabbi Wayne D. Dosick

TOWN HOUSE PRESS
Chestnut Ridge, New York

Library of Congress Cataloging–in–Publication Data

Dosick, Wayne D., 1947–
   The best is yet to be: renewing American Judaism /
Wayne D. Dosick.
      p.   cm.
   ISBN 0–940653–08–7
   1. Judaism—United States.   2. Jews—United
States—Politics and government.   I. Title.
   BM205.D67 1988   87–34742
   296'.0973—dc19   CIP

Printed in the United States of America

THE TOWN HOUSE PRESS, INC.
28 Midway Road
Chestnut Ridge, New York 10977

For

SCOTT and SETH

They, and their friends,
are our future

CONTENTS

Acknowledgments

I take great pleasure in expressing deepest thanks and gratitude to those whose influence is reflected in this book:

— the teachers of my youth: Rabbi Ralph Simon, Rabbi Benjamin Daskal, of blessed memory, Cantor Maurice Goldberg and Dr. Irving H. Skolnick, all of, or formerly of, Congregation Rodfei Zedek, Chicago, Illinois, in whose Synagogue I learned to *daven,* to sing Jewish songs and to love Judaism.

— Dr. Jakob J. Petuchowski of the Hebrew Union College, Cincinnati, Ohio, who taught me the integrity of scholarship; that it is still possible to talk about God in the modern world and that emotion and spirituality still have a place in this rational, intellectual age.

— Rabbi M. David Geffen, formerly of Congregation Beth Shalom, Wilmington, Delaware, now of Jerusalem, who gave me the first opportunity, and undeserved latitude, to "test my wings" and put academic theory into real-life practice.

— the members of Congregation Beth El, La Jolla, California, who taught me both the problems and the possibilities of the modern Synagogue.

— the men,women and, especially, the children of Congregation Beth Am, Solana Beach, California, who share the dream that the contemporary Synagogue can be a place of spiritual quest, intellectual growth and emotional fulfillment. They and our Shul are the "living laboratory" for the ideas in this book. I am profoundly grateful for their confidence, their trust, and, most of all, their friendship.

I am particularly grateful to Howard Goldstein, founding President of Beth Am, whose determination "made it happen," and whose brilliant legal mind crafted the structure; and to Peter Powell, the second President, whose commitment assures enduring foundations.

— my secretaries, Jeanne Steingold and Robbin Herman, who typed and re-typed and typed some more with unfailing skill and goodness. I promise. Next time, I'll use a word processor!

— my friends and colleagues, who listened as the ideas developed, read the first manuscript and graciously offered criticism and suggestions. They do not all necessarily agree with every idea presented here, but their insights and perceptions helped shape and sharpen my thinking. And, their own personal commitment to Judaism and its future assures that the issues raised here mean as much to them as they do to me: Dr. Gloria Fried, Professor of Education, Georgian Court College, Lakewood, New Jersey; Dr. George Fried, Professor of Biology, Brooklyn College; Dr. Joel Gereboff, Professor of Judaic Studies, Arizona State University, Tempe; Rabbi Menahem Herman, Congregation B'nai Israel, Tustin, California; Dr. David Lieber, President, University of Judaism, Los Angeles; Beth Carol Matez, formerly Director of Education, Congregation Beth Am; Michael Medved, noted author and lecturer, Venice, California; Rabbi David M. Posner, Temple Emanu-el, New York City; Dennis Prager, noted author, lecturer and radio talk-show host, Los Angeles; Rabbi Jack Riemer, Congregation Beth David, Miami, Florida; Alan M. Rubin, Professor of Student Development, Oakton Community College, Des Plaines, Illinois; Dr. Yehuda Shabatay, Executive Director, Jewish Community Educational Center, Portland, Oregon; Dr. Byron Sherwin, Vice President, Spertus College of Judaica, Chicago; Laura Walcher, President, Laura Walcher and Associates, San Diego.

I am particularly grateful to my long-time friend, Dr. Steven R. Helfgot, Vice President for Student Services, Cerritos College, Norwalk, California, for helping me to formulate the ideas that are presented here in the chapter entitled, "Planning Ahead."

— my literary agent, Sandra Dijkstra, for her wise counsel and for keeping the faith; and Alvin Schultzberg of Town House Press, creative and consummate professional, devoted and caring Jew, new and good friend.

— my parents, Hyman and Roberta Dosick, for their continuing encouragement, for their pride and for their love.

— and, most of all, my wife, Rona, for all that she is and all that she does; who walks with me hand in hand, whose love sustains me and whose compassion and warmth are felt by everyone she knows. This book is as much hers as it is mine, for she watched and prodded and comforted and smiled as the ideas were born, grew, tried, failed and succeeded. Her understanding and sensitivity permeate every page and her love for God and His Torah—and, thankfully, for me— are reflected in every word.

— and, finally, our sons, Scott and Seth, who always bubble with enthusiasm, with probing questions and with love; who understand, with a wisdom far beyond their years, what it means to share their father with a Synagogue and a community. We have watched and loved and cushioned and challenged, but, now, the butterflies begin to fly free and we can only marvel at their brilliant colors. There are only two lasting things that we can give our children: one is *roots* and the other is *wings*. We hope and pray that we have given both well.

Grow old along with me!
The best is yet to be,
The last of life, for which the first was made:
Our times are in His hand
Who saith, "A whole I planned,
Youth shows but half; trust God: see all nor be afraid!"

Robert Browning
in *Rabbi Ben Ezra*

Who I Am and
Why I Wrote This Book

My name is Wayne Dosick, and the highlight of my childhood was the year 1959, when the Chicago White Sox won the American League pennant.

Now, this may be a strange way to begin a book about Jewish life in America and new directions for Jewish survival, but I want you to know, right from the very beginning, that I am not some pious, other-worldly religious fanatic. I was not born a Rabbi, nor did I spend my youth in a dimly lit, overcrowded room, swaying over a Talmud text.

I was a typical American Jewish kid of the late 1950's and the '60's. For me, Little League was at least as important as Hebrew School, Saturday morning Services were locked into fierce competition with Saturday morning cartoons and Succot meant little more than a taffy apple handed out by a smiling Sisterhood lady.

No sudden flash of blazing light, no vision from out of the darkness, no mysterious, disembodied voice called me to Jewish life.

To be sure, I had some help along the way: parents who cared and showed, one or two less than boring Hebrew School teachers and a youth group which nurtured and offered opportunities to explore.

But, as I grew, I found in Judaism a sense of identity and belonging, authenticity and warmth. I came to marvel at a system of values that was created out of an incredible insight into human nature, an understanding of what people want and need, hope and feel. I found a

1

lifestyle that gives rhythm and structure to everyday existence; that brings explanation to the chaotic, beauty and meaning to the ordinary.

I found a religion and a People that affirms life with wordless melodies and confronts the mysteries and the wonders of existence with stories.

I became a Rabbi because I am a passionate lover of Judaism and the Jewish People. And, I have spent all of my adult life singing Jewish songs and telling Jewish stories and sharing the brilliance, the sensibility and the goodness of this faith with everyone I meet.

Therefore, you will understand when I tell you how pained and how frightened I am when I see that the Jewish community of the United States of America is in serious crisis and at a crucial juncture.

We stand between a recent past, marked by dazzling creativity with enthusiastic participation, and an unsure future, threatened by discontent, apathy and indifference.

For, despite the achievement of Jews in America— education, acceptance, affluence and influence—and despite the accomplishments of the last three decades: the serious scholarship coming from our Seminaries; the publication of thousands of books of Jewish interest; the popularity of our Day Schools, camps and youth programs; and the rise and growth of the Chavurah movement, the realities of contemporary Jewish life in America are disturbing and disheartening:

- The American Synagogue is in deep and serious trouble—often irrelevant and uninspiring, and, even more often, empty.

- The community organizations are fragmented and fractured by pettiness and politics and dominated by the demands of collecting money and fights over how to spend it.

- Most American Jews are "turned off"—staying

away and not participating: disaffected, disillusioned and disinterested.

- And, thus, the eternal Jewish message of Torah learning and Torah living is being ignored and, worse, lost under the clamor and crush of secular values and mundane pursuits.

What is at stake is our future: the quality of Jewish life for ourselves, our children and our children's children, and, ultimately, the viable, creative survival of Judaism and Jewish People.

In order to assure a healthy Jewish future, it is imperative that we immediately begin a raw, starkly honest self-evaluation of what is right and what is wrong with Jewish life in America, where we have succeeded and how we have failed.

That is what this book is about. First, it is a painful, deeply probing wrestling and struggling with what has been: a litany of our faults and our failures. Yet, there is no *tochacha*, no criticism and admonition, without the *nechemta*, without the comfort of suggestion and the hope of solution. After the warning must come the renewal. So, I will offer far-ranging, perhaps controversial, formulas and plans for what must be.

I am not a social scientist; I am not a scholarly academic; I am not a "think-tank" ponderer. I am a Rabbi who lives and works, day after day, year after year, "in the trenches," with you, with *amcha*, with Jews.

I listen to your nostalgia for what once was, but is no longer. I see your discomfort at being unfamiliar with Jewish rituals and Jewish teachings. I sense your bewilderment and your disappointment that organized Judaism does not adequately respond to your intellectual, social or emotional needs. I understand your desire to have the best that American life and lifestyle offer, while, at the same time, not completely abandoning the faith and customs of parents and grandparents. And, I feel your deep need for the sacred, and watch your tentative, halting steps toward Jewish life, even, if at first, it is "only for the children."

One thing has already become clear to me. Old forms, old "tried and true" responses and solutions to our problems are no longer adequate and will no longer work for you.

What is required is revolutionary innovation, newest technologies and techniques and inspired creativity. What is needed, here and now, is a complete transformation of Jewish life.

As I analyze and evaluate our recent Jewish past, and, then, struggle with the task of seeking out new directions for our Jewish future, I am guided and inspired by our Torah, which teaches:

"Remember the past, but understand the needs of each generation,"

and, by Bobby Kennedy, who was fond of quoting George Bernard Shaw:

"Some people see things as they are and say, 'Why?' I dream things that never were and say, 'Why not?'"

The Background

WHAT WAS

I grew up in the "golden age" of Judaism in America.

In the late 1940's, through the 1950's and into the early '60's, Judaism flourished in America as almost never before.

Even before World War II, the United States had been an extraordinary haven for the Jewish People. After centuries of fleeing from tyrant and persecutor and wandering from land to land, Jews found freedom, equality, opportunity, acceptance and human dignity in America. The early Jewish immigrants—those who came beginning in 1654—helped forge and fight for this country's independence. The immigrants who came in the early 1800's, from Germany and Central Europe, became leading businessmen and entrepreneurs and rose to positions of prominence and responsibility in industry and government. The flood of immigrants who came from Russia and Eastern Europe between 1880 and 1920— more than two million strong—lived the American dream. Within just two generations, the grandchildren of those poor, uneducated immigrants became doctors, lawyers, college professors, government leaders and top professionals.

To this land of promise, we Jews had brought commitment to Torah ideas: a systematic, ritual lifestyle to sanctify the everyday; an enduring code of moral and ethical behavior; a deep respect for knowledge and learning; a sense of justice and fair play; and infinite love and compassion.

The Jewish immigrant's passport into American society was simple: hard work, honesty and integrity and a public library card. Thus, from 1654 until World War II, Jews and America had many shared goals and aspirations, common directions and collective accomplishments.

But, as good as it had been before, *after* World War II, when I was growing up, any lingering doubts, any last barriers disappeared. Jews and Judaism were accepted in America, with virtually no question and no reservation.

We Jews had earned our place in American society. We had fought and died in the foxholes of Europe and on the battleships of the Pacific. The Jewish community was still the recipient of the sympathy of the world for the continually unfolding horrors of the Holocaust. We were all still caught up in the euphoria of the creation of the State of Israel and the decisive victories of her defenders.

With the exception of a real estate covenant here and a country club membership there, most all of the old impediments broke down. Jobs and professions that were once off-limits to Jews now put out the "welcome" sign. Businesses and corporations that had unwritten, but completely effective, exclusive employment policies, now competed to hire the best and brightest Jewish minds. The quota system disappeared, and Jewish youngsters were accepted into colleges and universities across the country. And, with the help of the G.I. Bill, Jews could now participate in the great American dream—owning a house in the suburbs.

In this atmosphere, it *was* American Judaism's "golden age."

The inner city neighborhoods were strong and vibrant. And, to every new town and suburb we went—you know them, because you moved there—The Five Towns; Main Line; Newton; Shaker Heights; Southfield; Skokie; the Valley—we built Synagogues and Jewish Centers.

The Hebrew Schools were full. Synagogue youth

groups were active. Institutions of higher Jewish learning were expanding and producing serious scholarship and publications. New Jewish Studies Programs were created in secular universities from coast to coast.

The neighborhood in which I grew up—the Southeast Side of Chicago—tells the story. In 1945, it was a Polish Catholic steelworkers' neighborhood, with no Jews and no Synagogues. By 1970, it was a black neighborhood, with no Jews and no Synagogues. But, in 1960, it was a neighborhood full of Jews, with two Jewish Centers and at least nine Synagogues, one of which had more than 800 member families!

From that one, small Jewish neighborhood, which was born and died in twenty-five years, I know twelve men who became Rabbis and countless others involved in Jewish issues and concerns.

Jewish life in America was dazzling, creative and very, very exciting.

But, then, something happened. Something went terribly wrong.

WHAT IS

Today, in the late-1980's, Jewish life in America is ill and ailing.

I know that statistics are only numbers, and often are wrong, and that they can be made to serve any preconceived purpose. But, statistics that are derived from serious, in-depth studies, conducted according to widely accepted scientific methodologies and standards, can help measure prevailing trends and attitudes. And, even if these statistics are off by five or ten or fifteen percent, they are still terribly frightening and very, very serious.

Emerging from a variety of studies conducted over the past decade, and succinctly summarized by Stuart

Eizenstat, former Special Assistant to President Carter, in his "State of World Jewry" Address, given in late 1981 at the 92nd Street "Y" in New York City, the reality of Jewish life in America today is:

- 70% of American Jews do not belong to a Synagogue. And, of the 30% who do affiliate, most do not participate with great regularity. Few Synagogues are filled to Yom Kippur capacity every Shabbat.

- Only another 10% of America's Jews belong to a Jewish organization, such as B'nai Brith or Hadassah, or make a contribution to a community agency or write a check for Israel.

  This means that a full 60% of American Jews have no formal affiliation with any Jewish institution or organization.

- 50%—one half—of all Jewish children of school age receive *no* formal Jewish education: not a Day School, not an afternoon Hebrew School, not even a one-day-a-week Sunday School.

- Somewhere between one-third and one-half (depending on whose statistics or studies you accept or believe) of all marriages involving one Jewish partner are mixed marriages. Up to one-half of all American Jews are marrying non-Jews.

- The Jewish birthrate has fallen to 1.9. We are the first and only ethnic group, anywhere, any time, to voluntarily reach zero population growth. We are not even replacing ourselves.

- And, perhaps most chilling, by many estimates, 20%–30% of the Moonies and the Hare Krishna are Jewish kids.

WHAT HAPPENED?

What happened to plunge our vibrant, creative Jewish community to the precipice of failure and self-destruction in such a short time?

In your absence and your silence, *you* give the answer.

If you own a business and you offer a good product at a fair price in pleasant surroundings with a friendly staff, and if you advertise your product well to make it appealing and attractive, then, your customers will buy and keep coming back for more.

But, if your product isn't good, or if people can buy something else somewhere else that is more attractive or lower priced or has a better salesman, then, your product will not sell and, eventually, you will be out of business.

The Jews of America, you, the "customers" of the Synagogues and community organizations, are telling us, the Rabbis, Educators, Agency Directors and lay leaders, that our product is not good. You are not coming to Shul. You are not educating yourselves and your children. You are not participating in Jewish rituals and observances. You are not giving to Jewish causes.

What happened to Jewish life in America? What are the central institutions of Jewish life, the Synagogue and the community organizations, doing wrong? What is so bad about the "product" that is being offered that so very few are coming to "buy"?

We must find out what's wrong with Jewish life in America and how to make it right again. If we don't, then, here, in this great land of freedom and opportunity, this Jewish community risks doing to *itself* what no tyrant has ever been able to do.

For almost four millenia, the Jewish People has survived and flourished. Neither guns nor ghettos nor gas chambers could destroy us.

But, now, *our own* apathy and indifference threaten to zap Judaism's vitality and endanger Judaism's future.

For, today, we flirt with the possibility that Judaism's 3,800 year old enduring tradition—and the promise of its creative survival—may wither and die in us.

So What?

Why all the concern? Why the alarm? Why the fear?

What would it really matter if Judaism disappeared? What difference would it make if the Jewish People were no more?

Perhaps the lack of participation and observance by most American Jews is the signal that a new age has dawned, that the enduring Jewish mission is now over—outdated and obsolete.

Perhaps the time has come for American Jews to fully integrate into the world, instead of setting ourselves apart.

Perhaps the time has come to stop emphasizing our particular uniqueness and celebrate, instead, our universal oneness.

Perhaps intermarriage and assimilation are not curses, but blessings, proving to us that instead of being separate and distinct, we can be "just like everybody else."

Nothing is worth preserving just for the sake of keeping it, or, even, because it has been around for awhile and it would be a shame not to have it anymore.

It would be hard to convince you, for example, that we need to preserve the Chevrolet. The Chevrolet is a car—better than some, as good as most, worse than others. But, it has no intrinsic value or inherent worth.

Is Judaism like that? Is it a religion and a faith community with no special qualities, no unique characteristics that justify its continued existence? Has Judaism outlived whatever usefulness it once had? Does Judaism no longer have any innate merit?

Should Judaism simply fade away—unmourned and unlamented?

Or, does Judaism have the substance and the significance that make it worth preserving?

What is Judaism?

Judaism is *ethical monotheism*.

Judaism has given us, and all humanity through us, the greatest standard of moral and ethical behavior that the world has ever seen. It is an ethical code of right and justice and goodness; a moral mandate that made quantum leaps beyond the norm when it was first spoken, and which has stood the test of the millenia, because of its brilliant understanding of the human condition.

Why has *this* moral code endured? Why have *these* principles survived beyond all others?

There can be but one answer:

The *author* of this moral code is *God*.

He, who created us, has declared how we, His children, must behave. God's commandments are not affected by situation or circumstance, not subject to whim or caprice. Right is right; wrong is wrong. And, there can be no argument, no dispute, no debate.

Since God's law is the source of how we are each to conduct ourselves, and, since Judaism is the means by which we learn and live God's word, then, without Judaism, we would have no way of knowing and continually remembering what God expects from us. And, the world would be plunged into moral anarchy.

And, Judaism is *ethical ritualism*.

Not only does Judaism give us the moral code by which to live, but, through a series of rituals and ceremonies, it gives us the *system* by which to perpetuate Jewish values.

A *mitzvah* is a command of God.

There are two kinds of *mitzvot* in the Torah: ethical and ritual.

The ethical—as we have just learned—demand that we behave in a certain way, that we conduct our lives in a moral manner. *Ritual mitzvot* revolve around the ceremonies and customs of Jewish life such as observing the Sabbath and Holidays, eating kosher food and praying in the Synagogue Service. Ritual *mitzvot* regulate our everyday lives and give rhythm to our daily existence.

What kind of *mitzvot*—ritual or ethical—do you think are more important?

It might be safe to assume that ethical *mitzvot* are more important, because Judaism's goal is to help us toward holiness, to show us how to sanctify our lives and our relationships through ethical actions.

But, actually, the Torah gives no indication that one kind of *mitzvah* is more important than the other. Ethical and ritual *mitzvot* stand side by side and we are told to "remember and do *all* the commandments of God."

So, Torah gives us not only the ethical and ritual *mitzvot*, but, also, the *system* by which *mitzvot* are to be observed.

A little child watches his parents light Shabbas candles *and* deal fairly in business; wear a *tallit and* treat a stranger with kindness; conduct a Passover Seder *and* give food to the hungry.

There is no distinction between the actions, because they both come from the same source—God. So, at the same time and with the same Godly authority, a child learns the habit of ritual, by imitating his parents *and* the habit of moral behavior, by imitating his parents.

Thus, Jewish ethics do not rely on individual definitions of "good;" do not count on whether or not you "feel like it;" are not dependent on the prevailing conditions of the day or the year.

Jewish ethics are bound up with Jewish rituals. And, so, you have not just a hope or a desire, but a foolproof method of knowing that not only you, but your *grandchil-*

dren will lead lives of Jewish values. If your grandchildren observe Jewish ritual—by going to Shul, observing Shabbas, celebrating Holidays—then, they will practice Jewish ethics and make Jewish choices too, because the Jewish *system* makes Jewish rituals and Jewish ethics inseparable.

And, the Jewish system works!

And, Judaism is *people*.

We are the people who found God and who stood with Him at Sinai. We are connected to each other's past, and we are committed to each other's future.

Our law guides us and our literature instructs us. Our language sets our cadence and our land affirms our roots.

Our calendar and ceremonies unite us and our songs, our foods and our dances identify us.

We are a people battered by despots and pummeled by persecution. But, we are a people summoned by destiny and touched by greatness.

What happens to one Jew—at any time, in any place—happens to every Jew; so being a Jew means a fair share of both burden and glory.

But, most of all, being a Jew means the sweetness, the joy and the incredible challenge of having a special, sacred mission.

What is our mission?

Our prayer tells us, simply and profoundly, that the Jewish mission is "to perfect the world under the Kingdom of God."

Ours is the task of living and teaching moral certitude, goodness, righteousness, justice, kindness, compassion and love.

Our job is to tell ourselves and the world, "There is a God, and He demands that you behave in an ethical way."

Our work is to do *mitzvot*, to follow and fulfill God's commands.

Our mission is to make the world a better place, to move it, step by step, closer to moral perfection.

So, now, understanding all this, ask the question again.

Is Judaism worth preserving and perpetuating?

There can be no question; there can be no doubt. The answer is a resounding, "Yes!"

For, without Jews and Judaism, the world would be darker and sadder; far less moral; far more corrupt.

Jews and Judaism keep the world from moral chaos and destruction.

Jews and Judaism bring the world toward wholeness and holiness.

It is not *Judaism* which has lost its worthy message and mission.

It is we *Jews* who have lost our way. And, it is the institutions of Judaism—the Synagogue and the community organizations—that no longer show us the way, or even inspire us to look for it.

It is time to understand what has gone wrong with Jewish life in America and how to make it right again.

It will be a painful self-examination and a brutally honest evaluation. But, it will be worth it.

For the reward is that we will find our Jewish soul, and be able to reclaim our rightful role as the inheritors and the transmitters of God's sacred mission here on earth.

What's Wrong?

THE SYNAGOGUE

ROLE—*The Synagogue, once purposeful and strong, is now desperately struggling to define its place and its function.*

What is a Synagogue?

We know the traditional three-fold definition of a Synagogue as a House of Prayer, a House of Study and a House of Gathering.

And, we have a great nostalgia for what we *think* the Synagogue *used to be*—my grandfather's *shtiebel*, my father's *cheder*, the close-knit neighborhood center of my youth.

The Synagogue *once was* the center of Jewish lives—the place not only to pray and learn, but to be with friends, to exchange news, to band together for a common cause, to watch children grow.

But the realities of modern life no longer countenance that kind of institution.

We live in anonymous skyscrapers in urban centers; in sprawling suburbs, linked only by miles of highway; in isolated rural and college towns.

Now, the Synagogue is a *building* to which we come at a specific time for a specific purpose and, then, leave for the next appointment, the next event in our busy lives. The Synagogue has become just one more place to go in our frenetic, modern lifestyle.

We live in a time of specialty boutiques—this one selling only a specific size of clothes, that one selling just one form of art. At the same time, it is a world of gigantic department stores and all-purpose malls. We do not know if the Synagogue should be a small specialty emporium, with fixed, limited offerings, or a huge general store, with everything for everybody.

We remember what the Synagogue used to be. We have some sort of misty vision of what it can be. But, we have not yet decided what we want it to be. In our confusion, instead of working to solve the problem of role and function, most of the time, we simply ignore the place.

WORSHIP AND LEARNING—*The Synagogue is failing to creatively fulfill its traditional role as a place of worship and learning.*

Those who lead the Synagogue have yet to realize that you will not come just because you "should."

In most communities, it is a very small minority of Jews who seek out a Synagogue because they feel compelled to *daven* three times a day or want to study sacred texts.

Yet, the Synagogue does little to appeal to you or to attract you with interesting, challenging, satisfying Services, classes and activities.

Most Services, in most Synagogues, are boring and uninteresting. Rabbis preach at you and Cantors sing at you. Classes are irrelevant to your lives and better social gatherings are taking place at the local country club.

The reality of modern life is that the Synagogue is in competition for your time, your involvement and your commitment with the vast array of entertainment and leisure-time activities that American life offers.

Why should a Jew, who is not personally committed

to Synagogue worship, come to a dull, uninspiring Service on Friday night, when he can stay home, instead, and watch the continually unfolding drama of "Dallas" on television?

The Synagogue has made a big mistake. It has remained a monolithic institution, saying, in essence, "If you want to be Jewish, then, you must come to me, for I hold all the truths that you should want. If you fail to come to me, it is not *my* fault. It is *you* who are wrong, because you are rejecting *me*."

At a time when Jews seem hungry for meaning and holiness, the Synagogue says, "Come, I will feed you. But, I am only serving an eight course meal, and that is what you must eat. If all you want is a sandwich or a salad or a cold drink, it is too bad. Eat what I offer, or go hungry."

The Synagogue does not touch you or respond to where you are, and, therefore, the Synagogue is empty, because you stay away.

HEBREW SCHOOLS—*Synagogue Hebrew Schools do not provide quality Jewish education for our children.*

Let's face it. Afternoon Hebrew Schools are terrible. They are up against incredibly bad odds to begin with. Children are tired after a long day of school and would rather be at Little League, ballet lessons or out playing. Most teachers have little training, and are overworked and underpaid. Most texts and materials are dull and uninteresting.

Meanwhile, our children are the "Sesame Street Generation." They learn to read from puppets and cartoon characters on television. In their secular studies, they use state-of-the-art equipment and learning aids.

Yet, we are still teaching Hebrew School the way it

was thirty and fifty years ago. The teachers have Israeli accents, instead of European; the textbooks have colored pictures, instead of black and white. But, in most places, the methods and methodologies are decades behind the times.

After five or seven years of afternoon Hebrew School, what have our children learned? How many can read Hebrew? How many know how to *daven*? How many have a sense of Jewish history? How many know specific Jewish ethics and values? How many are "turned on" enough to continue formal Jewish education after Bar or Bat Mitzvah?

The afternoon Hebrew School is one of the poorest of all educational forms. We are not quite ready to give it a proper burial, but we have not done very much to give it the infusion of quality and vitality that will help it do anything more than just limp along into another generation.

RABBIS—ature *The Rabbi's traditional role has been significantly changed and his authority and leadership have been greatly diminished.*

Many attorneys handle only one kind of law, in order to give the best advice, and most doctors specialize in one small field of medicine, in order to give the best care. But, the Rabbi is still expected to be everything to everybody— the expert on all subjects from *halacha* to Mid-East politics to interest rates on long-term loans.

Once the scholar, teacher and preacher, the Rabbi must now reconcile his (and, increasingly, her) traditional role with the emerging professional demands of being book reviewer, administrator and fund-raiser.

Once the master of Jewish law and ritual, the Rabbi now serves Jews who feel little obligation to fulfill the law, and, thus, have no need for the Rabbi's learning or authority.

So, when your doctor tells you how to get better, you heed his advice. When your accountant tells you how to file your tax return, you listen to his counsel. But, when your Rabbi tells you how to practice Jewish ritual, you say, "But, my Bubbie and Zayde did it differently."

Rabbis work long, difficult hours on an emotional rollercoaster, going from classroom to cocktail party, from *bris* to *shiva* house, all in the same day.

Rabbi Harold Kushner, of Natick, Massachusetts, and the author of the best-selling book, *When Bad Things Happen to Good People*, has described the Rabbi's life this way:

> "What our Congregations demand of us is that we do a lot of things fairly superficially and none of them terribly well, because doing any one of them well would take so much time and concentration that other things would be left undone. They want us to do one thing and immediately go on to something else, without having the time to finish the first or prepare for the second. We rush from a funeral to a wedding, to a sermon, to a class, to a counseling appointment, doing all these things faithfully and energetically, but never having the time or the capacity to stop and do one of them as well as we know it deserves to be done and as well as we believe we are capable of doing it."

Even in the midst of large numbers of people, the Rabbi feels isolated and lonely. There is a great distance between the lifestyle and commitments of the Rabbi and his congregants. He observes Shabbat and *kashrut* and Jewish Holidays, and, for the most part, they do not. So he is paid by the community to "be Jewish" *for them*, and, then, he and his family are continually scrutinized by congregants wanting to make sure "they do it right."

Who are the Rabbi's friends? Who are his buddies? With whom does he talk and laugh and cry?

The Rabbi's spouse and family live a "fishbowl" existence, subject to constant observation, a bevy of unwritten rules of conduct, and judgment, expressed and implied.

When you go to your doctor, you don't expect his wife to be in the examining room with him, and when you go to your lawyer, you don't expect her husband to sit in court to hold your hand.

But, even in this age of feminism, egalitarianism and two career families, congregants still expect to see their Rabbi's wife (or husband) in Shul for every Service and every program. After all, they say, if he advocates Synagogue attendance and participation in Jewish activities, how can his own wife not be there? And, his children are expected to attend Services, behave properly and excel at Hebrew School, and be the leaders of the Junior Congregation and Youth Groups. After all, say the congregants, if he preaches family values, shouldn't his own children be the prime examples?

The Congregation hires one person and pays one salary, but expects full-time participation and work from *two* people—the Rabbi and his spouse.

The unrealistic expectations and critical judgments of a Rabbi's family often mean heavy and harsh burdens and pressures which result in unhappy spouses, resentful children and frustrated, angry Rabbis.

He earns far less than his comparably educated professional counterparts in law and medicine, but, the very people he serves feel as if they own him, because they pay his salary.

The role of the Rabbi is part *Kohen*, gentle pastor, and part *Navi*, visionary prophet. His task is to comfort the disturbed and to disturb the comfortable. Yet, he is dependent for his livelihood on those whose lives he is attempting to change.

How does the Rabbi, who must pay his mortgage and send his children to college, have the courage and the ability to do not what is popular, but what is right, to say "yes" or "no" and really mean it without offending those who sign his paycheck?

Emotionally drained, lonely, frustrated by politics, trapped by repetitious work-loads and thwarted by low salaries, many American Rabbis have, in the last few years, left their pulpits. Some have entered related fields of teaching or counseling, some have made *aliyah*. As many have become lawyers, stockbrokers and real estate salesmen.

Maurice Lamm, widely respected Rabbi of a large prestigious Congregation in Los Angeles, distinguished author of many important works, explained his departure from the pulpit this way:

> "I cannot believe that a human being was en-
> dowed with talent to transcend himself, with
> galactic reach, with global vistas, with indefi-
> nitely variable capabilities—molded in the image
> of God—and all that was asked of him in his
> clock-bound existence, was that he repeat his
> workday success every day, endlessly, until he is
> Xeroxed to exhaustion. There simply must be
> something else to this life after you've done every
> project a dozen times. I must have some other
> talent buried in me. Is there no more challenge
> left in me?"

Another young Rabbi wrote a poignant farewell letter to his Congregation. He said:

> "When I first considered the Rabbinate as a ca-
> reer choice, I had envisioned a life in a quest of the
> spiritual values of Judaism in which my own
> personal life would serve as an example for the
> community. I would have time for my wife and

children. We would be able to serve not only as Jewish role models, but as role models for family life. One of the great ironies of the Rabbinate is that the reality is very different. In addition to the normal busy day, I am out of the house at least five nights a week. On weekends, I am sharing other people's joys and sorrows and am left with little time to enjoy my own children and create my own memories. So one of the main reasons (for leaving the Rabbinate) is to return to a more normal mode of life. As I told one congregant, I made the decision after I started listening to my own sermons."

No one is listening or responding to their professional frustration or their personal pain, and so we are losing the best and the brightest of our Rabbis.

At the same time, the American Rabbinate is, frankly, beset with a great deal of mediocrity and incompetency.

For all their professed modernity, our Rabbinical Schools still use centuries-old criteria to determine a potential Rabbi's qualifications—how much Bible, Talmud and Jewish law does he know? But the Schools do not adequately prepare their students for the multi-faceted, complex tasks of the contemporary Rabbi.

So, a new Rabbi enters a profession which requires knowledge and skill in communication, education, counseling, business and finance. But, he has little, if any, in-depth training in those fields.

A Rabbi is not required to take any kind of licensing examination to demonstrate that he can translate book knowledge into useful function. He serves no internship to hone his skills under the supervision of experienced practitioners. Throughout a career that may span thirty years or more, he is not required to take any continuing education courses or even, if he chooses, to open a book or read a professional journal.

There are, in the Rabbinate, sweet, good, kind men

who simply do not have the ability, the passion, the vision to inspire individuals or to lead communities. Yet, they continue, year after year, plodding along, never providing their Congregation with what it really deserves from a Rabbi.

And, there are men in the Rabbinate whose learning is shallow, who are poor speakers and boring teachers, who lack compassion and human warmth and who insult their people by never preparing and rarely caring.

Until there is, again, respect, joy and dignity in the Rabbinate, both *given* and *earned*, the Synagogue will be without direction and the Jewish community without effective leadership.

SPECIAL NEEDS—*The Synagogue is not recognizing and responding to a whole new set of human needs.*

There cannot be strong Torah, there cannot be strong observance or learning without strong, individual Jews. And, everywhere, today, there are individual Jews who are bewildered and confused, hurting and in pain. And, the Synagogue hardly sees them, yet less does much to help.

What is the Synagogue doing about:

- single parents and their children who do not fit into the "traditional" definition of "family,"

- divorced, non-custodial parents, who feel isolated and alone,

- single Jews who are looking for partners, or who want to be respected in their choice to be single,

- gay and lesbian Jews who want to be accepted for what they are,

- teen-agers who face hard life choices about drugs and alcohol and sexuality, and want advice and direction,

- the aged who are living longer than ever before and want to feel useful and productive,

- young couples, who haven't been in Shul since their own Bar and Bat Mitzvahs, but who now want to give their young children some kind of Jewish background,

- Jews by Choice, those who convert to Judaism and need acceptance and support,

- children who have learning disabilities and need special educational techniques to teach them about their Jewish heritage,

- the elderly left in the old neighborhoods, when everyone else moves to the suburbs,

- the Jewish poor, who live in a world where everyone thinks that all Jews are rich?

These are Jews who need the Synagogue for friendship, for comfort, for inspiration. What is the Synagogue doing for them—for us?

ADMINISTRATION—*The Synagogue is plagued by poor administration and ineffective business practices.*

If you ran your business the way most Synagogues are run, you'd be broke!

Most Synagogues are run by a democratically elected Board of Directors. This is, usually, a group of well-meaning people who are highly successful in their own fields of endeavor—law, medicine, business, teaching—but who know nothing about conducting a nonprofit religious organization, and who often know little about Judaism.

In small Congregations, these lay leaders try to "do it themselves," amateur, part-time volunteers running a day-to-day business. In larger Congregations, they hire an "Executive Director," for whom they have little respect to begin with. After all, they reason, if he is really a good businessman, why isn't he out succeeding in business, like we are, instead of working for our meager salary?

In almost every case, they hire a Rabbi to conduct the religious and educational programs of the Synagogue, but, because they assume that he is a "holy scholar," not to be bothered with mundane concerns, they do not give him administrative duties or power. Thus, the Synagogue is the only modern Jewish institution—including Federations, JCC's, Bureaus of Education, Family Services, Old Age Homes—where the top professional is not both the creative and the administrative director. The Rabbi is the titular head of the Synagogue staff, but has no authority over half the operation—administration and finance.

As a result, the business of the Synagogue is run something like this:

Let's pretend that I am sick and you are the doctor. I come to you and say, "Doctor, I don't feel well."

So you, the doctor, call in a group of, say, twenty people. In this group are four businessmen, three housewives, a Rabbi, two lawyers, a CPA, two university professors, a retired librarian, three teachers, a retired fisherman and two salesmen— all of whom have bodies and have been sick and have been well. But, there is no doctor or medical specialist of any kind in the group. Now, this group of people examines me and, after a lengthy meeting, they vote 12 to 8 as to the diagnosis of my illness. They would, then, vote as to how to treat me, but it's already late at night and most of the people want to go home. They might meet again tomorrow, but one of the businessmen has to go to Hawaii, the teachers have to go to school and the lawyers have to be in court. So, they delay their meeting until everyone can be present—nine days later.

At that meeting, two people call in sick. The remaining eighteen vote 11 to 7 how to treat my illness. Three of the seven in the minority are so sure that they are right, and so furious that their opinion was not adopted, that they walk out of the meeting.

Now, the remaining fifteen members of the group come to you, the doctor, and say, "We voted 12 to 8 as to what's wrong with this fellow. Nine days later, we voted 11 to 7 how to treat him. Now, Doctor, you accept our diagnosis and our plan for treatment and you do just as we say. Of course, if we are wrong in either diagnosis or treatment, then *you* are still responsible."

That is how most Synagogue Boards of Directors function and how most Rabbis must relate to their Boards. Without sound business practice, is it any wonder that Synagogues are fractured by politics and riddled with mis-management?

LEADERSHIP—*The leaders of the Synagogue often do not exemplify the goals of the Synagogue.*

To be a Synagogue leader ought to mean a commitment to religious observance and ritual—coming to Shul, taking classes, celebrating Holidays and Festivals. But, all too often, it does not.

Yet, instead of demanding the kind of leaders it deserves, the Synagogue is often forced to "take what it can get." The "Me Generation" of the 1970's and the "Yuppie Generation" of the 1980's, have meant a tremendous decline in volunteerism and community service. Good people are, simply, not coming forward to work.

The Synagogue exists as a faith community and the center of religious observance. Yet, so often its leaders are non-observant, non-practicing Jews. While they are to be lauded for their devotion and dedication to the institution, their leadership lacks credibility and force because their lives and choices do not reflect the Synagogue's purposes.

To make matters worse, being a Synagogue leader is no longer an honor to be sought and cherished. It used to be that the highest honor a community could bestow was a Synagogue Presidency. Now, the best people see the community organizations and, ultimately, the Federation itself, as the pinnacle of leadership and recognition. Instead of getting the most experienced and mature leaders, the Synagogue now gets people "on the way up" who merely use Synagogue work as a stepping stone to "bigger and better" things.

And, because the Synagogue is the "grass roots" of Jewish democracy, anyone who walks in and plunks down dues becomes a co-equal voice.

All too often, people who feel stifled or impotent at home or at work use the Synagogue as an outlet to hear themselves talk and to garner authority and power. Emotionally healthy people, who volunteer their time and energy to Synagogue life, can take the presence and pressure of these dominating authoritarians for only so long. Then, they walk away from the tension and the fights, leaving the leadership vacuum to be filled by the very ones who caused it.

Men and women of prominence and stature are not assuming roles of leadership within the Synagogue and the Synagogue suffers from the great void.

MONEY—*The Synagogue has great problems raising money and even greater problems deciding how to spend it.*

Synagogue dues and school fees, if they are to be kept affordable, simply cannot pay all the expenses that the Synagogue incurs.

Yet, the Federation, and international service organizations like Hadassah, B'nai Brith and ORT, and national Seminaries and institutions of higher learning have attracted the greatest percentage of donated dollars. Even though the Synagogue touches the most Jews at the most basic and individual levels, the Synagogue has very few people who give the large contributions that it takes to keep the institution functioning.

Further, a simple fact of Synagogue life is that people will give money for some things, but not for others.

It is much easier to collect millions of dollars to build a Sanctuary, which will sit empty except for five or seven hours a week, than it is to collect money to send youngsters to Jewish camp, or to bring scholars to teach, or to give Day School scholarships.

People would rather give to buy a *thing*—especially if the thing can have a contributor's nameplate on it—than give to develop *people*.

Are buildings our Jewish future and legacy? Where is money for Jewish hearts? Buildings will crumble in time, but a mind infused with Jewish knowledge, a soul infused with Jewish spirit, lives forever and ripples into eternity.

THEREFORE

From the moment it was created, the Synagogue has been the center of Jewish life and existence. From out of the Synagogue come the teachings and values that call us to touch the best within ourselves, and the absolute assurance that we are never alone in this world, because we have each other and we have God.

Now, the Synagogue is a hollow imitation of what it once was. We need to restore it and revitalize it, because everything that is ultimately important to us depends on it.

THE COMMUNITY

To compound the issues facing the Synagogue, the problems in the Jewish community are as bad, if not worse.

In more than two hundred communities across the United States, the Jewish Federation is the central agency providing Jewish services and raising Jewish funds.

The Federation is the modern embodiment of the early concept of the *kehilah*—the organized Jewish community which assumed the responsibility for the physical and spiritual welfare of all its inhabitants.

In practical terms, the Federation raises and distributes funds to support the modern State of Israel, a wide variety of national and international Jewish defense and social service organizations, and meets local Jewish needs through agencies such as a Bureau of Jewish Education, a Jewish Old Age Home, a Jewish Family Service, Jewish Community Centers, Jewish Day Schools, College Campus Programs and Community Relations Councils.

Yet, despite its increasing success at raising dollars and involving large numbers of Jews as supporters and workers, and despite its high international profile, in all too many communities, the Federation's theoretical principles and purposes are destroyed by practical disagreements over policies, political infighting and the ill-will felt between the leadership and those they try to lead.

There are five areas in which the Federation is floundering and failing.

SPENDING MONEY—*In almost every community, the Federation is Israel-oriented.*

A careful reading of the book *To Dwell in Unity,* by Philip Bernstein, Chief Executive Officer of the Council of Jewish Federations, from 1955–1979, tells the story.

Jewish Federations in the United States raise well over $650 million each year.

Each Federation decides how its monies will be divided between direct gifts to Israel and support of local agencies. The "splits" differ from community to community, but range from 50%–50% up to 70% for Israel—30% local, with the average somewhere between 60%–40% and 66%–33%.

How much of Israel's annual operating budget do you think is met by the $350–$400 million sent to Israel each year by the American Jewish community through the Federation campaigns?

10%? 25%? 17%? Less? More?

The truth is that all the Federation contributions from American Jews make up less than 5% of Israel's annual budget.

Now to be sure, that money is desperately needed by Israel. It goes for health services and immigrant resettlement and education and to build up development towns.

But, the reality is that the Israeli economy would not suffer greatly if the $350–$400 million it receives from Federations each year were reduced by $10, $20 or even $30 million. Yet that $30 million kept in local American Jewish communities—a few hundred thousand here, a half a million there—can mean the difference between a community that meets its obligations to itself or a community that fails itself.

No more than 8% of Federation-raised money goes for Jewish education in America, at a time when one-half of our children receive no form of Jewish education. No more than 1.5% of Federation-raised money goes for community relations in America, at a time when our Jewish community faces serious threats from the growing power of the Religious Right and a Congress and a Supreme Court that are constantly blurring the definition of separation of church and state. No more than 4% of Federation-raised money goes for care of the Jewish elderly in America, at a time when our Jewish population is growing increasingly older and living longer.

American Jewry is sending millions of dollars to Israel to put electricity into rural settlements and to buy soccer balls for border *kibbutzim*, while our own American Jewish population is not being creatively, or even adequately, served because of lack of funds.

Another few hundred thousand dollars kept in each local community could really make a difference. In growing Jewish communities, throughout the Sunbelt, those dollars can help provide services for burgeoning populations with many new needs. In established communities, those dollars can help maintain the level of services that is expected. And, in older, declining communities, those dollars can help stem the tide of shrinking services to diminishing populations.

Even though those who support Israel and raise money for her in Federation campaigns try to convince us that people would rather give money for T-shirts for a *kibbutz* soccer team than for Jewish education in America. American Jews cannot live our Judaism through Israel. We have to be strong and educated ourselves.

Going beyond his 1981 address, in early 1985, Stuart Eisenstat stated, "I truly believe we need a whole new Jewish agenda—one that focuses our priorities . . . . In the long run, *a strong, viable American Jewish community will help Israel more than annual donations from the United Jewish Appeal.*"

Supporting this position, albeit from across the

Atlantic, is the Chief Rabbi of the British Commonwealth, Immanuel Jakobvits, who once served as spiritual leader of the prestigious Fifth Avenue Synagogue in New York.

Early in 1985, Jakobvits stated, "In the face of astronomic financial needs for keeping Israel economically and militarily viable, *one or two million pounds more or less contributed by us will make precious little difference, but such amounts may make all the difference to the vitality or bankruptcy of Jewish life among the donors.*"

After 2,000 years of hoping and praying, we rejoice in the modern State of Israel and we passionately love and support her. But, has Zion become our only God?

PLURALISM AND ACCEPTANCE—*Even as American Jewry gives all this money to Israel, the Israeli religious establishment and government refuse to recognize the pluralism of modern Judaism.*

85% of the money raised in the United States for Israel is given by Conservative and Reform Jews, or those who identify themselves as "non-affiliated."

Yet, in Israel, controlled by the Orthodox establishment, Reform and Conservative Rabbis are not permitted to officiate at life-cycle events such as marriages. Conversions to Judaism performed by Reform and Conservative Rabbis in the United States are not recognized as religiously valid.

The Federation campaign slogan, "We Are One" is hard to accept when our money is good enough for Israel, but our religious practices are not.

HELPING ISRAEL—*In spending money for Israel, are we really spending it to her best advantage?*

One vote in the United States Senate for a weapons sale or a foreign aid package is worth more to Israel than all the money raised across the Jewish world in any year.

How do we fight for and protect Israel within the halls of our American government? In a political time when every "special interest" has its own issues, candidates and demands, how strongly do we stand up for our own needs and our own interests? How can we vote for a candidate who is not a passionate supporter of Israel, regardless of his "good" positions on other issues? What do we expect and demand from the Jewish members of Congress? How do we mobilize the Jewish community to influence Congress? With how much sophistication do we lobby?

The Federation supports an organized lobbying effort on Capitol Hill. How effective is it? How many votes and issues do we win or lose? What political consequences do we exact from those who oppose us?

We need to spend Jewish money for Israel where it counts the most—to influence the Congress of the United States to support her, to protect her and to preserve her.

Further, we need to spend Jewish money to help influence public opinion.

Israel takes a bad "rap" in the American press and on American television.

The Arab world spends millions upon millions of petro-dollars on propaganda, what they call "public relations," to help create a positive public opinion of the Arab countries and cause.

We spend little, if anything, to tell Israel's story. And, Israel is suffering. Public sympathy toward the Arab World, and negative feelings toward Israel, influence votes in Congress, give new hope and bravado to the Arabs, and discourage and dishearten Israeli and American Jews.

Jewish minds and money can help mold and form public opinion, but Federations spend few dollars on public relations or advertising, naively assuming that "moral right" will prevail. But, so far, it hasn't. We need to help Israel by telling her story and winning her friends.

RELATIONSHIP TO THE SYNAGOGUE—*There is a serious tension in the relationship between the Federation and the Synagogue.*

The central functions of Jewish life—worship, education and gathering—take place within the Synagogue. The great majority of American Jews who contribute to Federation campaigns are members of a Synagogue.

Yet, with very few exceptions, no dollars collected by the Federation are given to support Synagogue programs. Synagogue members, as a collective group, are expected to support the entire community's needs, but the community expects each individual Synagogue to make it on its own.

There is something very wrong with this arrangement.

LEADERSHIP—*The Federation honors and reveres people for what they give, not for what they know or do.*

The measure of a Jew is not how much he has, or even how much he gives, but how much Torah he knows and lives.

The Federation cannot make a mockery of Jewish life by giving positions of leadership to those who do not know an *aleph* from a *bet*; by electing Presidents who are married to non-Jews and by holding dinners to honor big contributors who treat Jewish ritual with disdain and violate Jewish ethics with impunity.

The time has come. We must have the integrity to say that a checkbook is not enough, but that we expect Jewish values and Jewish lifestyle from our Jewish leaders.

THEREFORE

It is a vicious circle. Because the Federation is plagued by all these troubles and controversies, potential participants in Federation programs and potential donors to Federation campaigns stay away and do not give what they otherwise might. And, when not enough money is contributed, the Federation cannot adequately provide the services it should.

It is a vicious circle that must be broken, because everyone loses.

The Consequences

What is happening to the Federation and the Synagogue means that the entire American Jewish Community is permeated by problems.

Far too few recognize the impending crisis, or are even willing to admit that it exists. Therefore, few, if any, creative solutions are being offered.

As a result:

OBSERVANCE—*We have, increasingly, non-observant Jews.*

Since I live in San Diego, I'll say this about my city, but I think it could be said about every American city where Jews live.

On any Friday night when the Padres are in town, I am sure that there are more Jews in San Diego Stadium watching the ball game than in all the Synagogues of San Diego County combined.

So much of Jewish life has become, for so many, a mystery instead of a *mitzvah*.

There are a few traditions and celebrations which are still widely observed: the High Holidays; lighting Chanukah candles; a special dinner on Passover; saying Kaddish for a parent. But, the core rituals of Judaism are largely ignored and forgotten.

Life-enhancing Shabbas, with its rest, rejuvenation, prayer, family closeness and joy has been replaced with "the weekend," when we run from activity to activity trying to entertain ourselves.

We disdain *kashrut* as narrowly particularistic and anachronistic, but we have become connoisseurs of pizza, French wine and moo-goo-gai-pan.

We celebrate Labor Day and Memorial Day and Washington's Birthday, but we can hardly draw the distinction between Succot and Shavuot, especially since both begin with the English letter "S."

Jewish rituals and observances, customs and ceremonies, used to give rhythm and flow to our People's days and years. Now, they are but a distant memory, relegated, by most, to relative obscurity, destined to be dusted off only now and then.

LEARNING—*We have, increasingly, ignorant Jews.*

Given a choice of spending one hour a week at a class on jazzercise or Spanish language or financial planning or Bible, the vast majority of American Jews choose anything but Bible.

The sad reality is that the "People of the Book" can no longer read the Book in its original language and rarely read it in the vernacular.

Our strength as a People has always been our commitment to learning, our passion for acquiring knowledge. Here, in America, we have become skilled surgeons, nuclear physicists and Ph.D.'s in French Literature. But, most Jews cannot read and translate a simple line of Hebrew. It is a tragedy beyond words.

CHILDREN—*We have Jewish children who are, increasingly, being denied their heritage by their very own parents.*

Twenty years ago, when, as a young student myself, I began to teach, I would say to a child, "This is the *bracha* your mother says when she lights the Shabbas candles." And, I would proceed to teach the words to the blessing.

Five years after that, I would say the same thing and children would say to me, "What's a *bracha*?"

Five years later, when I made the same statement, children asked me, "What are Shabbas candles?"

Now, when I say, "This is the *bracha* your mother says when she lights Shabbas candles," children ask me, "What's Shabbas?"

It is not the children's fault! They cannot possibly know something they have never experienced.

Children cannot be expected to learn or even care about Judaism, when their parents tell them, by word and by deed, that Judaism is not important, when it is "pigeon-holed" into a couple of hours called "Hebrew School" on weekday afternoons and when its customs and ceremonies are as foreign to them as Zulu tribal rites.

While most parents are not interested in much of Jewish life for themselves, they *say* that they want it for their children—up to a point. So, they send them to Hebrew School, as long as it does not interfere with soccer, Little League, ballet lessons and all the other "vital" activities that parents think make their children "well-rounded."

Yet, parents show their children their *real* attitude toward Judaism in just fifteen seconds a week.

When parents drop off a child at the Synagogue door for Junior Congregation on Shabbas morning and say, "Go because we say it is important," and, then, drive off to the tennis court, the golf course or the supermarket, their actions tell their children everything.

Nothing that the Rabbi or the teachers say or do in the six hours of Hebrew School a week can overcome the negative, or, at best, indifferent attitude and feelings about Judaism that parents pass on to their children.

And, if by some miracle of patience and fortitude, a child survives the years of Hebrew School and has a Bar or

Bat Mitzvah, the immediate decision, usually told to the Rabbi or Principal with the greatest of glee, is to "quit" Hebrew School. And, the vast majority of Jewish parents permit their 13 year old children to end their formal Jewish education, saying, "After all, he's a big boy now. It's his decision."

What parent would let a 13 year old child quit regular school; to stop learning math or English? What 13 year old child is old enough, mature enough to make such a life-affecting decision for himself? Yet, parents are willing to pawn off this vital decision onto their children because, truth be told, the parents don't really care.

Reb Shlomo Carlebach, the dynamic Rabbi-singer of our time puts it this way:

"Jewish Parents! If your child is not feeling well, you give him a bowl of chicken soup. And, if he wants a second bowl, who would deny him? And, if he gets sicker, you take him to the best doctor you can find. And, if his teeth need fixing, you take him to the dentist, to the very best dentist.

But, when your child's *soul* is sick, when your child's soul is empty, what do you do for him?"

Jewish parents are filling children's souls with soccer, with baseball, with computers and with parties. Who will teach them *Yiddishkite*? Who will teach them *menshlikite*? Who will teach them *rachmanos*?

No Jewish parent would deny a child his financial inheritance. But, Jewish parents are stripping away their children's spiritual heritage, the richness of their past and the promise of their future. It is not fair. Our children deserve better.

FAMILY—*The Jewish family is, increasingly, breaking down.*

It used to be that the Jewish family was the envy of every ethnic and religious group, the star of every sociologist's study. It was stable. It was solid. It was forever.

It used to be that if a Jewish child married a non-Jew, his parents would sit *shiva*, mourning for him as if he had died. Now, mixed marriages are becoming the norm. By many estimates, in up to one-half of all marriages where one partner is Jewish, the other is not. (This does not count marriages where one of the partners converts to Judaism before the wedding. That is a Jewish marriage.)

Love grows out of similar experiences, mutual mores and shared values. Here in America, millions of Jewish children have been reared without unique Jewish lifestyle, observances and value systems. Since Judaism is not a core component of their makeup as human beings, it is no wonder that they do not feel the need to seek out Jewish marriage partners.

The first tragedy of the Jewish family is that, time and time again, it is no longer being created. Sometimes, a non-Jewish spouse will see the beauty of Judaism and, at some point in the marriage, decide to convert. But, in most cases, not only one Jew, but his children and his children's children are being lost to Judaism forever. Mixed marriage is decimating the Jewish family and sapping the vitality of Judaism.

It used to be that Jewish men and women married early and soon had little Jewish babies who were the center of their existence. Now, Jewish men and women are marrying later or not at all.

For some, being single is by choice. For most, if truth be told and false bravado penetrated, it is an unhappy, lonely, undesirable place to be.

And, Jewish families, where four or six children were once not unusual, are now two children or one child or none at all.

It used to be that "other people's children" got into trouble; did poorly in school; took drugs; drank liquor; got pregnant.

Now, Jewish children are just like everybody else's children; confused by all the conflicts they face, but not being given any special direction or structure to help them make their choices.

As the divorce rate amongst the general population approaches 50%—that is, one in every two marriages ends in divorce—the Jewish divorce rate is not far behind.

Jewish marriages are crumbling and falling apart, leaving bewildered and angry ex-husbands and wives and sad children who are shuffled between warring parents.

It used to be that within the Jewish family love and nurturing, responsibility and sharing were born, experienced and nourished. Within the Jewish family, patterns for living and the truths and values of human existence were transmitted and learned. Now, the Jewish family is weak and falling apart, and the cost to the Jewish community and the toll in human pain and suffering are beyond measure.

SPECIAL PEOPLE—*We have, increasingly, ignored Jews.*

The sad truth is that the organized Jewish community does not know what to do for the proliferation of Jews with special interests and special needs.

We are bewildered by the high Jewish divorce rate; we are uncomfortable with single adults; we are embarrassed by the gays; we refuse to acknowledge disabled children; we are sure that drug and alcohol addiction cannot possibly happen to our kids; we can't handle our elderly parents; we don't know what to say to converts and we won't admit that there are poor Jews.

Unless people fit into a neat, preconceived mold, we most often ignore them rather than reach out to help them.

As a result, Jews with special needs are turning away from the Synagogue and the Federation, which do not respond to them, and are turning, instead, anywhere and everywhere they can find understanding, acceptance and help.

The Biblical promise, "My house shall be a house for all people," is just not true anymore. And, we are losing hundreds of thousands of Jews who feel unwanted and unloved.

MORAL LEADERSHIP—*We have an increasingly decentralized Jewish community, without collective voice or moral suasion.*

Do you remember the old joke about two Jews and three opinions? Unfortunately, it's not a joke.

The Jewish community of America no longer has any "giants"—leaders who are compelling moral visionaries who can rally us to great issues and great causes.

Instead, we have "fiefdoms." A whole host of agencies, organizations and self-appointed leaders compete with each other to carve out individual spheres of influence.

The organized religious community is divided into four "official" wings—Orthodox, Conservative, Reconstructionist and Reform. And, each group has whole sets of subgroups; left, right and centrist; liberal and conservative; mainline and fringe. Each of the wings and each of the subgroups within the wings disagrees with the others' positions on *halacha,* ritual and theology. Usually, polite public acquiescence to each other's existence prevails, but disrespect, distrust and disdain see the right below the surface.

Whatever *halachic* and moral authority Rabbis have is limited to their one small subgroup. So, unlike decades past, few, if any, great Rabbinic leaders have emerged to capture the imagination and respect of the entire Jewish community.

To fill the void left by powerless Rabbis, the secular Jewish leaders from the Federation and the array of Jewish organizations have stepped forward to try to set the agenda for American Jewish life. But, the religious community is not prepared to cede such power to the secularists, so, absolutely no consensus is reached.

As well, the secularists are beset with their own serious contradictions and disagreements. How can any one organization expect massive support? What is, for example, the best way to support Israel? Hadassah tells me to outfit hospitals, ORT tells me to build training centers. JNF tells me to buy trees. Magen David Adom tells me to buy ambulances. Who is right? Whom shall I believe and support? Where is the focus and direction and collective purpose for our American Jewish community?

Our fragmentation hurts us terribly.

In relationship to others, we are no longer fulfilling the Prophetic mandate to work for social justice.

Only two decades ago in the United States, the Jewish community was at the forefront of the civil rights movement, at the vanguard of the anti-war movement, leaders of the debate for civil legislation to feed the hungry, shelter the homeless, educate the illiterate and insure the dignity of each human being.

Lately, our voices are seldom heard. Today, it is difficult to name more than a very small handful of Jewish leaders who call us to work for the rights and hopes of others. We once marched and linked arms and went to jail with America's blacks. Today, there is a schism between the black and Jewish communities; many blacks distrust us and some of their leaders insult us and question our integrity. Not long ago, we passionately supported candidates whose platform was social justice. Today, we vote our pocketbooks instead of our principles.

Where is the voice of moral right rising up from the

Jewish community to call to us and challenge us to do right?

In relationship to the issues that affect us on the world stage, we are hurting ourselves and our causes.

To whom does the government of the United States turn when it wants opinion or position from the American Jewish community? Seeing no consensus, an Administration turns either to a "court Jew," who has earned his place more through contributions to a political party than by real credentials within the Jewish community, or to one or another of the organizations or agencies which, rarely, if ever, can speak with the voice of a *united* Jewish community.

Who amongst us would stifle free speech or freedom of expression? Yet, look where the freedom takes us and look at the harm it does. Not long ago, the President of the United States encountered Jewish demonstrators demanding more U.S. aid to Israel. Right across the street were pickets protesting Israeli settlements on the West Bank and demanding that all U.S. aid to Israel be withheld until the settlements are removed. Arab sympathizers, right? No. More Jews. Whom shall the President believe? To whom shall he listen? What shall he assume the American Jewish community wants? Without consensus, he will do as he pleases. So, our contradictory input neutralizes and leaves us ineffective.

We have seen the power that collective voice and actions can have. When we were most vocal on behalf of Soviet Jewry—demonstrating in front of the U.N., sending petitions and letters to Soviet leaders, influencing trade legislation in the American Congress—tens of thousands of Soviet Jews came out of Russia each year. But when our voices are quiet, when our protests diminish to a very few, only a few Jews trickle out of the Soviet Union.

When we kept our issues and concerns before the world, it made a difference. When we are silent, nothing happens.

Where is the voice of moral right rising up from the Jewish community calling us to protect our own interests, to best help our Israeli brethren, to do the work that it takes to bring our Soviet brothers and sisters from slavery to freedom?

And, within the Jewish community, our internal problems are going unsolved.

The observance of *kashrut* in the United States is rife with discord. Why is the quality of kosher meat so poor and the price so high?

There is no way, for example, that a soon-to-be-married couple (considering more and more ritual observance, but not quite there yet) will choose to have a kosher home when the prices for kosher meat are double and, sometimes, triple, supermarket prices. Why should Thanksgiving turkeys cost 59¢ a pound at the supermarket and $1.99 a pound at the kosher butcher?

Why aren't kosher butchers removing the sciatic nerve from the hind quarter, giving us the best steaks and, at the same time, effectively *lowering* prices, because more meat is available?

Worse, how do we face elderly Jews, on fixed incomes, for whom *kashrut* is a life-long commitment and a life necessity, when they can no longer afford the escalating kosher prices and are forced to do without?

When kosher meat is so expensive, Jews eat *treif* and one of the life-enhancing *mitzvot* of Judaism is "priced out" of practice.

Where is the voice of indignation and moral right rising up from the Jewish community to demand better quality and lower prices from our kosher butchers and suppliers?

And, why are Jewish burial costs so high? There is no reason that Jewish funeral and burial should cost a minimum of $2,000–$3,000. Costs *can* be kept much, much lower.

But, when Jewish funeral and burial costs are so high, Jews are using non-Jewish funeral homes and, worse, choosing cremation, violating the sanctity of life's final *mitzvah*—burying the dead with honor.

Where is the voice of indignation and moral right rising up from the Jewish community to demand lower funeral and burial costs in order to preserve traditional Jewish laws and customs?

God once asked, "Whom shall I send?" Who will go for us?" And, the Prophet Isaiah responded, "Here I am. Send me."

Who will go for *us*, who will speak for us in our time? Who will be our voice of moral right? And, if he or she speaks, will we listen?

We are being divided and fragmented by our own egos and selfishness and our Jewish community is without leadership and direction. We need moral giants with strong voices to lead us. And, we need to listen and follow.

ISRAEL—*We are, increasingly, challenged over our support for the State of Israel.*

Israel is the physical homeland of millions of Jews and the spiritual homeland of every Jew. To paraphrase the medieval poet Yehuda HaLevi, we are in the West, but our hearts are in the East—in Jerusalem, the city whose very stones bespeak her holiness.

Since Israel was reborn in 1948, we have lived with her, shared her struggles, rejoiced in her victories, built her with our hands, given her our hearts, supported her with our dollars and visited her time and time again.

We love Israel because, for us, she is mystical, spiritual, holy. But, we must deal with her in starkly real terms: as one nation-state among many; as a tiny beleaguered country in the midst of powerful neighbors who would destroy her; as an entity viewed by the world not in moral terms, but by political practicalities.

We passionately support the State of Israel and urge our American government to do so with financial aid, arms supply and votes in the United Nations. We must speak about her, therefore, not in theological terms, but in the language of politics. We remind that Israel is the only democracy in the sea of totalitarian nations. We describe her strategic importance to America's military. We point out that support of Israel is not just for her and for us, but is in the best interest of the United States.

For all our efforts, we are charged by our detractors with blind, uncompromisingly loyalty to Israel and with lack of sympathy for Arab nations and Palestinian refugees. And, when the crunch comes, there are whispers about our alleged "dual loyalty." When all else fails, our allegiance to America is called into question.

So, during the oil shortages of the 1970's, American Jews were quick and constant to point out that the crisis was not caused by Israel, but by the Arab nations' greedy desire to increase prices. We felt compelled to explain and disclaim so as not to be accused.

And, do you remember a few years ago when the U.S. Senate voted to sell sophisticated AWAC airplanes to Saudi Arabia? We lobbied against the sale, but it passed by a very close vote. Senator William Cohen of Maine (who is not Jewish, despite his last name) changed his vote at the last minute. He said that, while he opposed the sale, he voted for it, because he was afraid of the *potential backlash* against Israel and American Jewry if the sale vote failed.

Against his better judgment, Cohen was willing to put state-of-the-art military hardware in the hands of the Arabs, rather than put America's Jews in jeopardy. He must have sensed how deep the sentiment against us was running in his state and in this country.

To make matters worse, in the past few years, many American Jews have had serious questions about Israel's policies and actions. There is disagreement over West Bank settlements and Palestinian rights. We were in genuine conflict over the incursion into Lebanon. Yet, whenever we raise these issues, we are accused *by Israel* of disloyalty. We are challenged with all the usual, but probing, questions: If we are not there, how can we really know what is going on? What right do we have to question the decisions of her government? How dare we criticize Israel's means of protecting herself the best way she knows? What Jew lives in the Diaspora when he could live in Israel? Come, we are told, be with us, help us. Live where you belong.

We feel caught in the middle between our loyalties as Americans and our loyalty to Israel. It is a difficult and an uncomfortable place to be. And, whenever we try to reconcile the delicate balance, either Israel or America won't let us.

THREATS—*We are, increasingly, threatened by outside, external pressures.*

It seems hard to believe, but, by most estimates, 20%–30% of the Moonies and the Hare Krishna are Jewish kids.

The cults are swooping down and taking our children and we seem powerless to stop them.

What is it that the cults have that is so intriguing, so appealing, so alluring that our children are forsaking family, friends, background and lifestyle to dress in sheets, sit on the floor chanting nonsense syllables and venerate gurus and swamis?

Rabbi Harold Schulweis, one of the seminal Jewish thinkers of our time, suggests that there are two reasons that our youngsters are captivated by the cults.

First, he says that the cults are nothing more than fancy street gangs. They use street techniques and street methods to attract members to live in packs by offering protection and comradeship.

But, our children, who are brought up in the golden

ghettos of upper-middle class suburbia, have no street smarts. They are easily conned by smooth talkers and smooth operators. In street terms, they fall for the oldest tricks in the books.

The second reason Schulweis gives for our kids going to the cults is much more painful and more damning.

Schulweis argues that, without meaning to do so, and even without knowing we are doing it, Jewish parents give Jewish children *conditional* love. We say we love our children. We would do anything for them. And, accused of anything less than greatest love and affection, we would vehemently deny any guilt.

But, Schulweis says, we do it anyway. Subconsciously, we give our children the message: "I love you. But, I will love you even more *if* you get straight A's, *if* you marry a Jewish boy, *if* you become a doctor or a lawyer instead of a truck driver or barmaid."

The cults, on the other hand, offer *unconditional* love. Their members physically surround a potential recruit and say: "We love you. We care about you. Moon or Krishna or Swami loves you. We don't care who you are or what you are. We love you just for being you. We don't care if you are a thief or a dopehead or flunked out of school. We love you. And we will take care of you. And, we will protect you. And, we will love you, always."

This, says Rabbi Schulweis, is how the cults appeal to our kids.

To his two reasons, I would add a third. Young people, today, are desperately searching for something beyond themselves and the good life they have been handed. They are searching for the spiritual, for the eternal, for the reasons for being, for a power greater and mightier.

All of these things exist, of course, right in Judaism. But, *we have failed to show* our children Judaism's beauty and sense, its answers to the mysteries of the universe, its warmth and love. So our children turn elsewhere seeking, and they wind up in the cults.

We are losing many of our young people to cults and

gurus. We have to get them back—for themselves, for us, for our future. And, to get them back, we have to be ready and able to give them what they are seeking.

More threats. The America in which we live is, on one hand, an increasingly secular society.

The highest paid workers are not the doctors who heal us or the teachers who mold young minds or the clergy who guide and comfort. We offer astronomical financial reward to the entertainers who tell us jokes and the athletes who play children's games. We work very, very hard at entertaining ourselves and, when we aren't having fun, we run from counselor to therapist to find out why.

The average American watches $6\frac{1}{2}$ hours of television every day, while the television industry tells us that its programs are geared, on the average, to the intelligence of a 12 year old. Hard drugs are peddled on elementary school playgrounds and cocaine is offered with the hors d'oeuvres at suburban cocktail parties. Drunk drivers litter our highways with their carnage. And so many of the values of our society are shaped by *Playboy* and *Penthouse*.

It is an extraordinary challenge to live and teach our children Torah values in a time and place where "eat, drink and be merry" and "wine, women and song" are not just quaint old phrases, but, for so many, the goal of existence.

On the other hand, a small, but passionate and vocal minority is trying to Christianize America.

The fundamental Protestants, the Religious Right of America, have a clear agenda. They want to shape America according to Christian teachings and Christian values.

They seek a Constitutional Amendment banning abortion. They seek a Constitutional Amendment permitting prayer in the public schools. They support, with votes and big dollars, political candidates who agree with them. They work to defeat political candidates who oppose them.

The Congress and the Supreme Court hear the footsteps. The Court has recently permitted a nativity scene, erected with public funds, to be placed on public grounds in celebration of Christmas. The Congress has recently enacted "equal access" legislation, permitting religious groups to organize after school clubs on public high school campuses.

The Religious Right holds burnings of books they don't like, calls rock and roll music the "work of the devil" and organizes little schoolchildren into "armies for Jesus."

So, where does this leave the Jews? The Rev. Bailey Smith made it clear. "God," he said, "does not hear the prayers of the Jews."

To the Religious Right, we Jews are condemned sinners. Our only salvation is to accept Jesus. Their mission is to save us. But, failing that, they ignore us. We are no more than a slight irritation.

First Amendment rights? Separation of church and state? Pluralism? A land of religious freedom and choice?

Forget it! says the Religious Right. The only way to save America, they claim, is to Christianize it. And, if we Jews object or get in their way, they will plow right over us. We are just a small stumbling block on their path to righteousness.

America's Jews—our faith, our beliefs, our practices, our rights—are under attack. Today, the attack is fairly quiet and subtle. It would not take much to make it overt and insistent. And, so, we must be constantly on guard.

To compound our problem, overt acts of anti-Semitism still take place in the United States.

Synagogues are still vandalized. Cemetery tombstones are still overturned. Graffiti are still scrawled.

So far, these incidents are separate, individual acts, seemingly unlinked by any unified plan or conspiracy. But, they are symptomatic.

The fact of history is that every great nation that has ever existed on the face of this earth has, eventually, fallen. Sometimes, nations were vanquished by more powerful armies. Many other times, nations decayed, crumbled from within and destroyed themselves.

The second fact of history is that before the final destruction of every nation, a scapegoat was found to blame for all the troubles and failure.

The third fact of history is that if Jews were living in a crumbling nation, Jews were the scapegoat.

Nations decay from the inside for a number of reasons. William Gibbon, in *The Decline and Fall of the Roman Empire,* lists four: corruption in commerce and government; excessive spending on amusement; breakdown of family; and decay of religion.

Add to these the financial factor. When a country's economy is bad, then, jobs are scarce, children are hungry and people are left homeless. They are afraid and very angry.

Sound familiar?

It would be naive to assume that what has happened to every other great nation throughout history cannot happen to the United States of America.

And, just like any other nation, before the United States would crumble and fall, it would need and find a scapegoat. And, when it comes to being a scapegoat, we Jews know what it means to be the chosen people!

Outside forces, external pressures, seem to be buffeting us at will. We must be constantly on guard, because they could destroy us. And, we must try to find controls and solutions, so that we can be the masters of our own fate and our own destiny.

VALUES—*We, increasingly, fail to remember and live traditional Jewish values and ethics.*

The ultimate mark of a Jew is not where he lives, or what he wears, or, even, what he eats or how he prays, but how he behaves.

All of Judaism—the rituals and observances, the customs and ceremonies—is for but one purpose: to teach us the ethical mandate by which to shape our lives.

But, no longer steeped in Jewish learning, no longer enveloped in Jewish ritual, we have forgotten:

- that honoring parents and not oppressing strangers and caring for the orphan and respecting the elderly are not just polite gestures, but the only right and just way for people to treat each other;

- that dealing with decency in business and not cheating or lying or deceiving; paying a fair wage and doing honest work are not dependent on the whim of the marketplace, but are daily imperatives;

- that *tzedakah* means that we give not because the IRS offers tax breaks, but because it is the sacred obligation of human beings to share with each other.

When morality is tailored to the situation or the moment, people become capricious and cavalier. But, the great universal ethics of Torah have transcended time and space because they define obligations, demand respect and assure the dignity of every human being.

To live and not teach God's life-enhancing moral values is to abandon the covenant which Abraham found and Moses forged. Sinai is ever present, except when we forsake it.

THEREFORE

The consequences of our actions in our Federations, in our Synagogues and in our homes are clear. We are slowly and tragically destroying ourselves and the Jewish future.

Enough! There is too much at stake. There is too much to lose.

Let's find out the reasons why all this has happened and let's see what we might do to give ourselves new hope and new promise.

The Reasons Why

From this exploration of Jewish life in America, one thing has become very clear. The Synagogue and the community organizations are *not meeting the needs* of the Jews they are supposed to serve. Therefore, Jews are staying away from the institutions and seeking meaning and human connection elsewhere.

Why?
Where have the Synagogue and the community organizations failed?

The Jewish institutions of the late 1940's, the '50's and the early '60's helped all of us achieve our successes as American Jews: acceptance, education, affluence, influence.

But, now that we have those successes, the institutions have not grown with us.

The Synagogue and the community organizations have not adequately *responded to* or even *understood* the tremendous revolution that has taken place in American life in the last twenty years.

It used to be that the pendulum of history swung slowly and deliberately. Eras in human development took hundreds of years to unfold and be played out. But, now, the world moves in bold, dizzingly swift strokes.

Throughout all human history, there have been but two great epochs—the agricultural age and the industrial age. We live on the cutting edge of a new time, as the industrial age gives way to history's third era: the information age.

The making of things is being surpassed by the sharing of ideas. The world is linked by satellite and instant communication into what Marshall McLuhan has called the "global village." Our neighborhood is now the entire universe.

It is an incredibly exciting time to be alive.

As the world changes, human needs change rapidly too. In the late 1940's and the '50's, people sought out each other to help attain shared goals and aspirations. Mutual support meant strength given and received, collective ambitions realized.

In the 1960's people were ready to reach out beyond themselves, to help others deemed less fortunate or more needing. "We Shall Overcome" became the rallying cry of the decade.

But, the altruism of the '60's caved into the selfishness and the self-centeredness of the 1970's. After having given so much to others, the mantra became, "Me. Me. Me."

Now, what about the 1980's? Some will simply merrily continue the selfish individualism of the '70's. Others will try to turn the clock back to a rigid, narrow life-view. But, for most, it seems as if we are heading for a synthesis and a blending of the preceding years.

The new technologies and scientific advances will give individuals more time, more freedom, to make choices. Individuals will cherish and protect their own preferences and pleasures, but, at the same time, will want to reach out to others in order to feel a sense of connection and community.

The unfolding image of the late 1980's and the 1990's is of strong, self-confident human beings, standing with arms outstretched to touch each other's fingertips, holding hands in a circle of friendship and mutual nurturing.

As John Naisbitt put it in his pathfinding book,

Megatrends, it will be a time of "high tech and high touch."

The Jewish institutions of the 1940's and the '50's provided the sense of community for shared aspirations, and, in the 1960's, led the way toward the fight for social justice.

But, the Jewish institutions of the 1970's were embarrassed by the selfishness and turning inward. And, in the 1980's, they have no idea of what is happening to you, what you are feeling or what you want.

So, the first reason that Jewish life in America is ill and ailing is that the *Jewish institutions have failed to understand and respond to the new realities of the world in which we live, and the new needs of the people they should be serving.*

The second reason that Jewish life in America is in deep and serious trouble is that, even with all our seeming integration and acceptance, *we Jews have not yet comfortably defined ourselves or found our place in America.*

Despite all the good things we have achieved, there is a conflict and a tension in our lives that is unresolved. *We do not yet know who we are or what we want to be.*

The glitter of American affluence and influence pull at us from one side. We cherish the open society that permits us to buy houses in the fanciest suburbs and send our children to Ivy League universities. We like the things that money can buy. We relish the influence we have with politicians, with whom we are on a first-name basis.

But, old loyalties, old observances, old moralities tug at us from the other side.

As much as we want it to be otherwise, as hard as we try to convince ourselves that it is, *we have not yet been able to happily and maturely integrate into American life.*

There is about us a duality, a split personality, a schizophrenia.

We would like to know and observe Jewish tradition and customs. We would like to give our children the education and values they deserve. But, we cannot decide if Harvard is our Sinai and New York our Jerusalem.

We would like to take care of the people in need and hear the voice of morality and right directing our community. But, we no longer feel comfortable with the role of the ancient prophet. We could once march with the blacks, but, today, we are afraid to tell the kosher butcher that he must lower his prices. We have a hard time taking care of ourselves, and an even harder time reaching out to others. Striving for social justice is no longer popular or easy in the midst of boardroom affluence.

We would like to do our best for Israel, and suppress the threats that challenge us in America, but, we still feel vulnerable enough to worry about those who assail us and not secure enough to oppose those who attack us.

The truth is that we would like it both ways. We want to have the best that America offers and the best of Jewish life—all at the same time.

But, we are learning that it is not that simple.

We are moving further and further away from our authentic role of knowing, learning, observing, loving, committed Jews. And, we know that we are suffering for it.

So, we stand on the precipice, straddling the canyon. We are unwilling to move one foot or the other to either side, yet we know that we cannot remain this way for too long, lest we lose our balance and fall to the sharp rocks below.

So, what are we to do?

Some will tell you that the only way for Judaism to survive is for you to forsake all the allures of materialism and secularism and to immerse yourself in Jewish life.

That is a dramatic plea, but, it will not work, and, besides, it is not right. A few may choose this way, but they will be on the fringe; isolated and alone.

Others will tell you that there is no hope for Jewish life

and Jewish survival against the onslaught of materialism and secular values. So, give up the fight, give in and enjoy.

That, too, makes a dramatic argument. But, it is not right either.

What *is* right is that we Jews, like our world, stand on the brink of a new era for Jewish life, an era which we can carve out and create for ourselves.

Creating The New Era

Judaism teaches that human beings have free will and self-determination. We are not puppets or automated robots; we grow, evolve and can change. When we make mistakes, we can correct them; if we have problems, we can find solutions. If we have failed, we can pick up the pieces, try again and succeed. We are in charge of our own lives.

Instead of letting what is wrong with Jewish life in America overpower us, let us see what it will take to create a new era in which Jewish life can be healthy and right again.

Rabbi Chaim Potok, the popular modern historian and novelist, teaches that the richest and the most creative times in the history of our civilization have been when the core elements of one culture—its definition of reality, its responses to the central questions of existence, its system of values—encounter the core elements of another culture. The diverse components of each culture meet in tension, but, rather than one culture sweeping away the other, the two fuse into something new.

This creative merging has happened twice in Jewish history.

Biblical Judaism, in which the Jewish People was born, grew out of the tension of the power of the pagan world and the emerging Jewish life-view of monotheism and sacred values.

In the heat of the desert, Judaism forged its own

61

theology and lifestyle. There were some clear "no-nos," prohibitions against participation in pagan rites and rituals that were non-negotiable mandates. Yet, Judaism understood the lure and the potency of the pagan world and tried to work with it rather than against it.

So, some customs and activities of the pagan world were appreciated, taken in, internalized, sanctified and Judaized.

For example: Jews did not invent circumcision. It was a rite used by almost every ancient Semitic tribe as either a birth offering to the gods or a ritual of sexual initiation. But, it was taken into Judaism, given special new meaning as the sign of the covenant between God and His People. And, circumcision has survived the centuries as a uniquely Jewish ceremony.

Another example: the Bible writers did not invent the poetic form of the Psalms. It was, originally, a Caananite literary mode. But, to someone else's model, the Psalmist brought Judaism's own soul cries of anguish and joy. And, the Book of Psalms survives in the Hebrew Bible as an incredible contribution to the religious poetry of our world.

Biblical Judaism taught the benefits of living with our neighbors, maintaining our own integrity, but not isolating ourselves or denying ourselves all the worthwhile things to be learned from the culture around us.

The second time in Jewish history that creative tension between us and our neighbors brought great benefit was the period of Rabbinic Judaism.

No time in Jewish life has ever been fraught with more danger and potential for disaster. In a 400 year period, from 200 BCE until 200 CE, look what Judaism faced: the Greek and Roman influence in the Land of Israel and the military rule that slowly wiped out rights and sovereignty; the Syrian takeover of the Holy Temple; the birth and death of Jesus and the rise and growth of Christianity; the destruction of the Temple, the plunder of the land, the end of independence and the exile of the people.

Any *one* of these events would have been enough to wipe out any group of people. But, Judaism survived them all.

For, from out of that time of challenge to Judaism came: the Maccabees, who led the world's first military uprising for religious freedom; the growth of the Synagogue, so that worship by means of animal sacrifice could be replaced by worship through prayer; the evolution of the scholar-Rabbi to replace the cultic Priest; the writing of the Mishnah, the code of law that created the tools for survival in an alien land and an hostile environment.

Again, Judaism maintained its own integrity and its own uniqueness, but it interacted with the society in which it lived and met the challenges that the society presented. Judaism synthesized what it found and devised new forms which permitted it to survive and reach new heights of creativity.

That second era of Jewish history built the foundations on which Judaism would survive the next 2,000 years—the ability of Judaism to adapt to its environment, responding to all the challenges, accepting the best that the host culture has to offer, all the while holding fast to its core beliefs and practices.

Now, we stand on the brink of a third Jewish era. Instead of being swallowed up by the secular values that threaten to engulf us and strip away Judaism's special uniqueness, we can be part of what Potok calls Judaism's encounter with secular humanism. He says:

"At some future time, eyes will gaze upon us. They will perceive that we were once in an interface between civilizations. And they will say of us that we used our new freedom—the freedom for which we hungered but were never fully granted by Europe—either to vanish as a people or to

re-educate ourselves, rebuild our broken core
from the treasures of the past, fuse it with the best
in secularism and create a new philosophy, a new
literature, a new world of Jewish art, a new
community, a third civilization of Jewish people.
That is the adventure that lies before us."

It can be done. We can assure the creative survival of
Judaism. By blending the best of two worlds, we can find
a healthy new way to live as Jews in America.

As in times past, we will have to maintain the integrity of who and what we are, celebrating and protecting
our distinctive life style and values. But, at the same
time, we have to recognize and appreciate the American
culture in which we live. Rather than fight against it, we
can work with it to create a synthesis of Jewish tradition
and contemporary reality.

We will take from America the best that it has to offer,
integrate some of its modes and forms and shape a new
Jewish future. We will be enriched as individuals and as
a People and we will save Judaism, not as it has been, but
in a new, reconstituted form.

If Jewish life and the Jewish future mean anything at
all to you, then, you have no choice. If the institutions of
Jewish life have become fossilized and have not met the
new needs of American Jews, then you must fix those
institutions.

After all, a Federation is not files, telephones and
campaign manuals, and a Synagogue is not an Ark, a
Torah and an Eternal Light. The Federation and the
Synagogue are the people—you and me—who make them
up. We the people created them, nurtured them and
ruined them. Now, we the people must fix them.

But, if by some chance, the people who currently run
those institutions are so entrenched, so intractable, that
the institutions cannot or will not change, then we—each
and every single one of us—have to save Judaism *for
ourselves, by ourselves.*

It's never too late, but, it's never too soon. Jewish history and your own satisfaction as a human being are waiting.

So, let's begin. Let's find the solutions and make the changes that will save us.

Finding Solutions and Making Changes

THE COMMUNITY

NEW REALITIES

Even with all its troubles, the Federation has a lot going for it. The Federation has an important role: the tasks that it undertakes must be fulfilled in order for a community to meet its responsibilities to itself. The community *needs* a central voice and a coordinating agency. No one wants the Federation to fail. Everyone is "rooting" for it to succeed.

All the problems the Federation has *can* be solved because all the problems stem from the same place. In order to overcome the challenges that are currently tearing it apart, the Federation needs to *understand the people* it purports to serve and *respond to the realities* of their lives.

It is a different world from the one in which the Federated community was born and began its work.

When the Federation was created in the last years of the 19th century, it met a clear and present need: to centralize, under one umbrella organization, the social welfare activities of the Jewish community and the efforts to raise the funds to support those activities.

The traditional responsibilities of the Jewish community for education, care for the elderly and infirm, feeding the hungry, sheltering the homeless, providing for the wayfarer, dowering the bride and burying the dead would all be met by one, unified agency. And, instead of having to make twenty small donations to various "causes," a Jew could fulfill his obligation to his community by making a single large *tzedakah* donation which would, then, be divided amongst the full range of communal needs.

Throughout the years, from the Federation's beginnings until well after World War II, those who were asked to support the Federated community understood its purposes and responded to its requirements.

Today, a new generation of Jew has grown up in America. Variously described as "baby boomers" and "Yuppies," this is a group of people ranging in age from late 20's to early 40's. Well-educated, professionally successful, increasingly affluent, and, in the majority, involved in Jewish life in only a marginal way, this generation does not know the structure of the Federated community or understand the role and the function of the communal agencies. What was basic assumption only a generation ago is now completely unknown.

So, the first task of the Federation is to *recognize* its new constituency and, then, to *inform and teach* about its work.

What does a Federation really do? What is the relationship between a Federation and a Bureau of Jewish Education? a Jewish Old Age Home? a Jewish Family Service? a Jewish Community Center? What is the relationship between the local Federation and the national United Jewish Appeal? How does money given in Oregon or Texas make its way to Israel? What does Israel do with our contributions?

The answers to these questions may have been general knowledge a generation ago, but, today, to this generation, not only are the answers unknown, the questions do not even occur.

So, the Federation must become an *instrument for Jewish education*—to teach a new generation about the structure of the Jewish community and the vital humanitarian role played by its organizations.

In order to do this, the Federation must conduct attractive, stimulating, challenging programs and activities which will inform, inspire and involve. These programs must go beyond the old "lecture series" or "information nights," and must be created to appeal to the intellect and the emotions, to the senses and sensibility. No modern marketing, advertising or educational technique can be spared in order to "sell" the work of the Federation and its agencies to a new group of consumers and supporters.

The "generation gap" is also manifest when it comes to giving.

Since so many positions of Federation leadership are based on years of experience and amount of contribution, current Federation leadership is dominated by people in their late 40's, 50's, 60's and 70's—people who have "worked their way up" and who have enough money to make major donations.

These people, by and large, grew up during the Depression and the war years in the United States. They can still raise money on feelings of demand and guilt by saying to each other, "We didn't have. Now we do. We must give."

At the same time, these are people who well remember a world before the establishment of the modern State of Israel. They can raise money for her by evoking memories of the struggles for Statehood, the euphoria of her creation, the many battles she faced. "Do you remember the night we sat around the radio listening to the United Nations vote? Do you remember the War of Independence, Sinai, the Six Day War? After all that, how can we let her down now?"

But, so many of the young people filling up Jewish America today have had every material thing we needed and wanted all our lives. And, for us, Israel has always been a reality—never more than an EL AL ticket away.

For this generation, the old Federation techniques, the old emotional appeals, the old arguments, will not work, either for raising money or for engendering commitment and loyalty.

Because of the great mobility of our society, few still live in the "old neighborhood," and many do not even live in the city of birth. There are no "old boy" ties, no one to come and say, "I knew your father, your grandfather. They were generous and giving, and I know that you will want to follow their example."

It is no longer enough to make an emotional appeal for Israel. The relationship cannot be automatically assumed, and, if we really want, we can get on an airplane and see her realities firsthand.

It is no longer enough to ask for funds for a Jewish Old Age Home. We have parents who winter in Florida, Arizona or Southern California and can afford the best care when they need it. It is no longer enough to talk about the counseling role of the Jewish Family Service. We go to the best psychiatrists and therapists when we need help. It is no longer enough to want to build a JCC to have a swimming pool and a gym. We belong to the finest health spas and country clubs.

This is a new generation of Jews in a new time, with new attitudes and new needs. The old appeals do not move us. The old techniques do not touch us.

The Federation must, therefore, *respond to the new realities* of the Jews whom it serves and from whom it seeks support.

These are Jews who will not give "just because," but must be shown why. These are Jews who do not necessarily have a relationship with Israel or with a local Old Age Home, but must have one created for them.

The Federation can no longer be just a fund-raising organization; the Federation can no longer just ask Jews for something. The Federation must *give* Jews something. And, what this generation of Jews wants is a true understanding of purpose, a sense of belonging and identity, a sense of personal involvement, a sense of needing and being needed.

So, at a time when so many Jews are staying away from Jewish life, the Federation must become a *transmitter of Judaism's tenets and values*. At a time when so many Jews are alone and seeking, the Federation must *offer community and involvement*. At a time when "giving" has come to mean "charity" based on profit and loss, the Federation must *convey the sacred obligation of tzedakah*.

Further, the Federation must give people the *opportunity for creative expression*, for giving of self. A woman who has spent years in medical school cannot simply be asked to pour tea and serve chocolate chip cookies. A man with an MBA, who handles millions of dollars in market transactions each day, cannot simply be asked to count cards. People want to share their talents and skills, and be appreciated for who they are and what they know. People want to give more than money and they want to get more than a computerized letter of acknowledgment.

Instead of having hands out, the Federation must have arms around shoulders. Then, partners in the process will respond generously to the collective needs of the community of which they feel a creative, sharing part.

Then, the problems that the Federation has can be solved.

SPENDING MONEY

Let's pretend. Let's pretend that you have $10,000 that you have decided to give to Jewish institutions and organizations this year. You now have to choose how you will divide your $10,000 in contributions.

You have many choices. There is no dearth of Jewish causes seeking your support. You can give your money to any one or all of these places:

- United Jewish Appeal for Israel,

- The operating, endowment or building funds of your Synagogue,

- The Jewish Community Center,

- The Jewish Family Service,

- The Bureau of Jewish Education,

- The Jewish College Programs on your community's campus,

- Jewish Day Schools,

- The national institutions which train Rabbis, Cantors and Educators for your branch of Judaism,

- The regional summer camps sponsored by your branch of Judaism,

- The local Jewish hospital and the research agencies for Jewish genetic diseases,

- A scholarship fund for youngsters to attend Jewish summer camps, take trips to Israel and study at the national seminary,

- Local, national and international Jewish service and defense organizations for their work in the United States and Israel.

How will you spend your $10,000?

I have posed this very question to groups of people in various parts of the country at least twenty times in the past ten years. And, each and every time, in each and every place, the answers are always the same.

The top *three* choices (not always in the same order) have always been: the Jewish Old Age Home, the Bureau of Jewish Education and the Synagogue funds.

The thousands of individual Jews with whom I have played this game of pretend have always chosen to contribute to and support local institutions and causes: their own Synagogue, care for the Jewish elderly and Jewish education.

Yet, the community-wide organization—the Federation—to which these people contribute their real dollars, spends for them far differently. The significant majority of Federation dollars goes to Israel and not to support local needs.

How do you really want your Jewish dollars spent?

The Federation spends tremendous amounts of time and energy convincing you to give, soliciting your contribution and collecting your money.

Now, the Federation must spend time *listening* to you. You *can* tell the Federation not simply that you will give money, but how you want your money to be spent.

The fact of life is this: the *giver,* not the collector, holds the real power. You—not some small "faceless" committee—decide where you want your Jewish dollars to go. The era of "big daddy" controlling the purse-strings is coming to an end. A new generation of giver and spender is emerging.

If the Federation will not respond, then the consequence is clear. You will stop giving your money to the community "pot" and start giving it directly to the organizations and institutions whose purposes and programs you wish to support.

Faced with diminishing participation and revenues, the Federation will have but two choices. Either, it will fall apart because it is no longer in touch with the desires of its constituents. Or, in the midst of new realities, the Federation will hear you, respond to you and work with you.

Then, if people who care are willing to listen to each other, reason together and struggle with difficult choices, the Federation can, once again, take its rightful place as the social conscience of the community.

When the Federation hears the will of the people, it will, once again, become not the master, but the servant of the people.

EXPANDING SERVICES

In addition to educating its constituents and re-aligning its spending choices, the Federation must begin to serve new groups of people and new needs with new programs and more funds.

It is no longer enough to support the "traditional" communal tasks of Jewish education, recreation, caring for the elderly and counseling the troubled. The Jewish community is now faced with new challenges which require solutions, and new groups of people who deserve attention.

If the Jewish community is interested in encouraging Jewish marriages, then the Federation must provide places, other than bars and "meat market" dances, for the growing numbers of Jewish singles to meet.

If the Jewish community is interested in Jewish couples having Jewish babies, then the Federation must provide decent day-care centers so that working parents can have comfortable places and skilled, nurturing people to care for their children. And, it must provide significant financial aid so that any child who wants it, can have a Day School education and summers at Jewish camps.

The Federation must help the elderly who are left in the "old neighborhood" when "everyone else" moves to the suburbs. Programs such as kosher co-ops, meals-on-wheels, financial counseling, daily telephone visitations, adopt-a-grandparent, visiting medical personnel and a host of others, need to be instituted and upgraded. Our seniors—our parents and grandparents—cannot be forgotten, nor can they just be given an occasional speaker or hot lunch.

The Federation must help fashion and form new communities in new places. Sun-belt cities and suburbs are rapidly filling up with new Jewish residents who are desperately seeking friends, a sense of identity and a few of the expected Jewish amenities from "back East." Instead of focus and direction, these people are usually left on their own, offered little more than a "Newcomers Party" and a booklet with long lists of information. Here is "new ground" that the Federation—in cooperation with the Synagogue—can break. How does a Jewish community grow "from scratch"? What does it need? What services should be provided? How do people come together to articulate their common goals? What can the organized community do to make people feel comfortable, cared for, involved? The best thinking and the most inspired creativity that the Jewish community has, must go into seeking the answers to these questions, for, in these new places, the foundations for the future are being built.

There are others whom the Federation must notice: Jews by Choice, single parents, young families. They all need recognition of their special status and a community that cares and provides for their needs.

The Federation is now confronted with the necessity of identifying and understanding the myriad of new needs within the Jewish community, providing expanded services to meet those needs and finding the resources to pay for the services. How the Federation meets this challenge will determine whether or not it will have any meaning and relevancy to the lives of individual Jews in the years and decades ahead.

RELATIONSHIPS: WITH ISRAEL

If the power is with the giver in relationship to the Federation, then, the power is with the Federation in relationship to Israel.

Ever since the establishment of the State of Israel, the American Jewish community has been told by Israel, "We need your support and your money, but, please do not interfere with our internal affairs."

Every time issues of religious pluralism and recognition of Conservative and Reform Judaism have been raised, every time we have tried to influence the internal process and the decisions of the Jewish Agency, which distributes American contributions in Israel, we have been told, "Now now. Please. The time isn't right to discuss those things. We are in the midst of (choose one or more): war; cease-fire; inflation; economic recovery; delicate negotiations with the Arabs; a workers' strike; elections. Later, when things are calm, we'll talk about your needs. But, in the meantime, keep sending money."

The problem is that "later" has never come.

If the American Jewish community is to be an effective partner with Israel, then the partnership must be based on equality and mutual respect.

We can no longer have our money accepted, while our Rabbis, religious practices and sincerely-felt political views are rejected.

We hope that Israel will listen to us because the Judaism which we live and teach is valid and vital and deserves respectful attention and admiration. We hope that Israel will listen to us because our business and management practices, experience and expertise have much to offer. But, if our reasoned positions will not be heard, then, the time has finally come for our money to talk.

It has been long enough being told, "Sha. Be still." It has been long enough that our money has been good, but our Judaism and our opinions not.

Ted Kanner, the farsighted Executive Vice President of the Los Angeles Jewish Federation Council, has put it in clear stark terms:

> "The next five years will see dramatic changes in relations between American Jewish philanthropy and Israel. Today's lay leaders are getting ready to play hardball. They're not your traditional storekeepers. They're corporate managers, who understand clear objectives and will have less and

less patience with bull. . . . Partnership means more than writing a check."

As harsh as the reality may be, the time has come to tell Israel, "Listen to us. Deal with us. Address our issues. Accept the reality of religious pluralism, the validity of non-Orthodox Judaism, the true partnership between giver and receiver. Or, face the risk of losing our financial support."

It won't be long before religious recognition and respectful consultation come.

RELATIONSHIPS: WITHIN AMERICA

The television newscast shows scenes of rubble left from a bombed-out building. Women are wailing, men look dazed and little children are milling around in tattered clothing. The reporter solemnly intones: "This is the devastation caused by Israel's latest incursion into Southern Lebanon. Left homeless, these children have no place to sleep tonight."

As the anchorman reappears on the screen, he slowly, sadly shakes his head. His sorrow over the destruction and the plight of the poor children is evident to every viewer.

Once again, the American public has been given a view of Israel skewered by the prejudices of the American media.

For, what the camera *failed* to do was pull back twenty feet to show not just the one building, but the whole area. If the camera *had* taken in the whole scene, it would have recorded pictures of the inhabitants of that little town cheering the Israeli soldiers and throwing flowers in their path in gratitude for having liberated them from the terrorists who had controlled their village for ten years or more.

Wars are not won on the battlefield alone. Wars can be won in the mind's eye and in the public perception.

And, for too long, Israel has been losing the war of American public opinion because of the massive Arab propaganda campaign and the built-in bias of American television, newspapers and news magazines.

If we, in the American Jewish community, really want to help Israel, then it is time that we use significant amounts of Federation collected money to help influence and mold public opinion on behalf of Israel.

We need not make up any stories or do any false advertising. We just need to tell the whole truth, so that Israel will no longer be hurt by the partial truths told by a single lens camera held by a single-minded reporter.

We need to tell the American public that Israel is the one bastion of democracy in a sea of totalitarian governments; that Israel is America's one ally in keeping the Soviet Union from taking over the Middle East; that Israel has made the desert bloom and has given the world tremendous technological achievements; that Israel has taken in the homeless of all faiths and creeds; that Israel respects and cherishes the religious rights of all people and gives its Christian and Moslem populations complete self-determination, without civil interference, in matters of personal status; that Israel maintains free access to the holy sites of all religions; that Israel provides free education to all its children, Jew and Arab alike; that Israel gives complete rights of citizenship to all its people, including its Arab minority; that Israel is a wonderful place to visit and warmly welcomes tourists.

Some of the best, most creative minds on Madison Avenue belong to Jewish people who use their skills to sell dog food, breakfast cereal and blue jeans. These Jewish minds have to be put to work and given the budget to tell Israel's story in 30 and 60 second television and radio spots and in print ads in newspapers and magazines. They *can* do it, and Israel will benefit immeasurably.

Israel needs good will and favorable sentiment in the court of world opinion and, particularly, in the United States. So, our investments in Israel cannot be only for social services in the cities and play equipment on the *kibbutzim.* Our investments must be made where they count the most.

Let's use our Federation dollars to Israel's very best advantage. Let's tell her story and win her friends.

And, let's find the ways to use our money where it really counts the very, very most: to influence votes for Israel in the Congress of the United States.

Since the Federation is a tax-exempt organization, regulated by the United States Government, and since contributions to the Federation are tax-deductible, the Federation is limited, by law, from engaging in political activities. Only a small percentage of Federation funds can be spent on lobbying or in attempting to influence legislation.

Yet, it is very clear that so much of Israel's existence and viability depends on votes in the United States Congress for military equipment and direct financial aid.

So, how do we influence our Senators and Representatives to vote favorably for legislation beneficial to Israel? How do we use our resources to get the very best help for Israel from our American Government?

There are six ways.

First, the Federation *does* maintain what it calls the Washington Action Office. With its expenditures limited by law, it, nevertheless, does a very credible job of making the wishes of the American Jewish community known. We need only to make sure that the Federation continues to fund that office to the limits permitted by law and engages the best, most savvy people as our spokesmen.

Secondly, there is great power in the postage stamp and in the telephone call, for our Senators and Representatives do care what we think, how we feel and what we want.

Since the average American Jew cannot be expected to know the intricacies of foreign aid packages or arms sales to Arab governments or church-state subtleties, the Federation needs to spend as much as necessary—and more—to keep the Jewish community constantly aware of the issues that are before Congress, of the votes that will be taken and of the Congressmen who need prodding. Through telephone squads, community alerts, announcements in Synagogues, radio, television and newspaper interviews and special mailings, each Federated community must continually tell its people what is happening, the implications and consequences of particular legislation and how and when to be in contact with Congress.

And, then, the members of the American Jewish community—each and every one of us—need to "keep those calls and letters coming" so that our elected representatives know what we want.

Thirdly, every American Jew needs to know about AIPAC, the American-Israel Public Affairs Committee. AIPAC is the registered lobby of the State of Israel. Over the years, it has been very effective in influencing Congress on behalf of Israel. Virtually every Senator and Representative knows of AIPAC and has felt the power of its influence.

Needless to say, much of the success of AIPAC is in direct relationship to the amount of money it has to do its work. The more lobbyists, the more lobbying. The more funding and support, the greater the perception of power.

Contributions to AIPAC are not tax-deductible, since AIPAC is not a nonprofit organization, but an arm of the Israeli Government. Yet, every dollar counts, so, if you would give a $100 tax-deductible contribution, give $50 instead. And, if you must, for personal financial reasons, reduce your contribution to Federation in order to support AIPAC, then, so be it, because AIPAC is the most proven and effective way to influence the Congress of the United States on behalf of Israel.

Rapidly emerging as a dominant force on the American political scene are the Political Action Committees, known as PAC's. Each PAC usually concentrates on one single issue and because contributions to PAC's are tax-deductible and the amount of money they can raise and spend unlimited, PAC's have tremendous power and influence.

A number of PAC's have been established to lobby for Israel and American Jewish issues. They deserve our attention and support for all the good they can do.

Next, we need to show our government leaders the realities of the modern State of Israel.

A number of Federations invite their local government officials to go on a seven or ten day mission to the Land of Israel. There, they travel the country, meet the people and talk with government leaders.

These journeys teach vivid lessons. No American politician who has stood in former Syrian bunkers on the Golan, staring at *kibbutzim* that were once the targets of constant Arab shelling or has driven from the pre-1967 borders on the West Bank to the Mediterranean, the short nine miles that could have cut Israel in half, can fail to understand the need for permanent and secure borders. No American politican who has stood at Yad V'Shem and at the Western Wall can fail to know the agony of a people at Auschwitz or the joy of that people reborn, with its ancient, holy city reunified. No American politician who has stood in an underground shelter with a mother and her babies, can fail to feel the anguish of war or Israel's determination to live in peace.

When an American politician has been to Israel, heard her story, seen her sights and met her people, then Israel has a new friend and supporter.

Over the years, the San Diego United Jewish Federation has sent many local leaders—the Mayor, City Councilmen, County Supervisors, the Chief of Police, newspaper editors—on missions to Israel. They came back knowledgeable about Israel's concerns and problems and enthusiastic advocates of her needs. Two of those City Councilmen are now members of the United States House of Representatives and that Mayor is now a United States Senator. Those three men are amongst Israel's greatest friends and supporters in the Congress of the United States.

The investment of Federation dollars to bring American government leaders to Israel is repaid hundreds of times over in goodwill and friendship. It is an investment well worth making.

Finally, the ultimate power with members of Congress is at the ballot box. Our Senators and Representatives need to know that American Jews are deeply concerned with issues we consider vital: support for Israel, the emigration of Soviet Jews, the separation of church and state, the protection of First Amendment freedoms.

If our needs are not met, if our desires are not heard, if votes favorable to us are not cast, then, like every other special interest group in America, we will answer with our votes. Every politician in this country must be put on notice. The so-called "Jewish vote" is not to be taken for granted. We will make no campaign contributions, we will not vote for any candidate who does not support the issues that are important to us. We have very specific needs in the political arena and only those who respond favorably to our agenda can count on our support.

Let's go to where the real strength is. Let's use our money and our influence for Israel—and for all the issues vital to Jewish life in America—at the apex of power. Let's make sure that when the American Jewish community needs, the Congress of the United States listens and responds.

RELATIONSHIPS: WITH THE SYNAGOGUE

The Federation and the Synagogue are the two primary institutions in Jewish life in America. Yet, instead of cooperating and working together, the Federation and the Synagogue are often divided by competition and jealousies and work at cross purposes.

Much of the friction and tension is a result of how the

Federation treats the Synagogue and how the Synagogue permits itself to be regarded.

The time has come for the Synagogue to no longer be the "pour cousin" of the Jewish community. While every other Jewish institution and organization—some with very narrow, limited purpose—receive community funding through the Federation, the Synagogue—which touches the most Jews and has the greatest influence on their lives—cannot be left to raise all its own money and fund all its own programs.

Each Synagogue cannot be expected to depend on its own members, alone, for all its support, for the Synagogue serves all Jews, without regard to affiliation, and meets all Jewish needs, without regard to compensation.

Therefore, every Federated community must, immediately, designate a significant percentage of its annual allocations to local Synagogues.

With greater funding, the Synagogue will be able to reach more people, meet more needs, teach more children. With greater funding, the Synagogue will be able to experiment with new ideas, create pilot programs, enter into new areas of activity, all of which will, ultimately, benefit every Jew in the community.

The discrimination must end now. The Synagogue not only deserves, but is entitled to its share of community funds. Practicality dictates it, for the members of Synagogues—who contribute the greatest portion of Federation funds—will insist on it. And, fairness demands it.

It is in everyone's best interest for the Federation to help fund Synagogue programs and activities. Both the Federation's mandate and the Synagogue's purpose will be better fulfilled. And, every Jew will be better served.

LEADERSHIP

Because of the new generation of Jews which is filling America today, a new kind of Federation leader is emerging.

First, the new Federation professionals—the Director, the Associate and Assistant Directors and the staff people—will no longer be just social workers with Jewish interests. These new professionals will be knowledgeable, observing Jews, who have specifically chosen work with a Jewish organization because of their personal commitment to Jewish ideals and Jewish survival.

The new lay leaders will have a clear sense of purpose. They will know what they want and create structured plans to meet their goals. They will want to know about Israel and want to understand the needs of the local community. They will manage money in a business-like manner and take seriously their accountability for spending it. They will hear the diversity within the community and work to respond to it.

They will do these things because, even if they are few in number, new Federation leaders will feel a sense of responsibility to Jewish life and service. And, yet, they will not have unlimited hours to spend with community work, nor will they waste time with pettiness or politics. They will be leaders who reflect the new needs and the will of the community they serve.

Even as this generation of leaders arises, it will impose upon itself serious standards of leadership. Leaders are no longer those who just write checks. So:

In order to be knowledgeable and informed about their role and responsibility, all Federation leaders must participate in formal study sessions to learn American Jewish history, the history and growth of the Federation and the history of their local Jewish community.

In recognition of the necessary bond between the Federation and the Synagogue, all Federation Board members must belong to a Synagogue and have served in at least one position of leadership there.

In order to demonstrate commitment to Jewish life and values, all Federation Board members should attend Synagogue Services regularly and participate in fixed periods of Jewish study each year.

In order to understand the relationships within the local Jewish community, all Federation Board members must have served on the Boards of at least two community agencies before coming to the Federation Board.

In order to know the needs of Israel first-hand, all Federation Board members should have already visited Israel or make a pledge to travel there within the first three years of Board membership.

In order to feel the obligation to the community at large, all Federation Board members must be annual contributors to the United Way campaign.

In order to keep Federation leadership fresh and vigorous, all Federation Board members must agree to serve on the Board for no more than five consecutive years and, at the same time, be directly responsible for bringing at least one new person into Federation work and potential Board membership.

Any organization is only as good as its people. The Federation is benefiting from the new breed of professional and lay leader which is now emerging.

The real proof of their effectiveness and success will come if those leaders have the courage to demand of themselves high standards of commitment, participation and involvement. If they do, then the Jewish community will have leaders of whom we can be justly proud.

THEREFORE

If, today, the Federation did not exist, undoubtedly, tomorrow, meetings would be called to create it, because the work it does is so desperately needed.

So, instead of letting the Federation destroy itself because of unpopular choices, or, simply fade away because it is out of step with those it is supposed to serve, let's work to fix it.

The process will be difficult and, often, painful, but the results will be very worthwhile. For, a newly revitalized Federation—clear in goals, responsive to the needs of

its people, programming creatively and spending wisely—
will bring new energy and renewed strength to the American Jewish community.

THE SYNAGOGUE

For 2,000 years and more, the Synagogue has been
the instrument of Jewish survival, the.place where Jews
have come to sing praises to God, to learn His word and to
share in each other's lives and concerns.

Today, the Synagogue is failing, and Jewish lives and
commitments are being abandoned.

It is now time for revival and rebirth, so that the
Synagogue can reclaim its rightful role, and lead Jews
back to Torah, Mitzvot and Ma'asim Tovim—Jewish
Learning, Jewish Living and Jewish Loving.

WORSHIP

Where are the best, the most exciting, the most
vibrant religious Services conducted?

The answer is simple: at Jewish summer camps like
Ramah, the Union-Institute and Yavnah; at youth gather-
ings like USY, NFTY and NCSY and in a few Junior
Congregations.

Youngsters sing and learn together, clap hands to the
music, grasp shoulders and sway to the melody and feel
the joy of *davening*.

And, then what happens?

They come home to their own Synagogues, where the
Service is coldly formal, where they are sung at and
preached to and where no one smiles at them. And, they
are turned off.

So, the question is: is there life after Camp Ramah or
a NFTY convention? Can we translate the warmth, the joy
and the excitement of those kinds of Services into our
Synagogues and into our daily lives?

Finding a positive answer to this question will determine whether or not most American Jews will ever come to Shul anymore.

The answer to the question began as a halting, tentative "yes" some twenty years ago.

The original Chavurah Movement grew up from people my age—graduates of Ramah, USY and LTF—who no longer liked what was happening in their cathedral-like Synagogues. So, they got together—first on college campuses, and, then, in urban settings—and made their own *minyanim,* where they *davened,* sang, clapped, learned and shared. If their Synagogue could not help them, then, they would do it for themselves.

What they found was that modern worship and prayer can still be a fulfilling spiritual experience.

The affirmative answer to the question got louder when Synagogues throughout the country began to hear the reverberations and permit small groups of people to use the Synagogue facilities for their own *davening.* While the "regular Service" was being conducted in the "Main Sanctuary," the "Alternative Service" or the "Chavurah Service" or the "Learner's Minyan" was taking place in the Chapel or the Library or the Auditorium. While the Synagogue was not ready to change, it, at least, recognized the new and different needs being expressed.

Then, slowly, the revolution began to take hold. The answer to what kind of worship must take place in American Synagogues is beginning to resound loudly from coast to coast.

The camps, youth groups, the early Chavurot and the original alternative Services taught us. For you to *want* to come to Shul, you must feel personally involved. You must feel intellectually challenged and learn something new each time you come. You must feel the emotion of *davening,* the sway of the melody, the spiritual connection. You must feel a relationship to the people you meet week after week, form friendships and forge commitments.

By now, the camps, youth groups and Chavurot have had a profound effect on Jewish life in America.

First, they have shown us that if the prayer-institution, the Synagogue, will not respond, then individual Jews can be intensely Jewish *for themselves, by themselves*.

And, secondly, they have been responsible for a transformation of the American Synagogue, itself. For, a whole new generation of Rabbis, like me, are the children of USY, Ramah and the Chavurot, and we are bringing to our own Synagogues the vitality of that kind of *davening* and learning.

The best thing that someone can do after a Service in my Shul is to smile broadly and say, "I enjoyed it." For, from enjoyment comes continued participation, dawning understanding, growing joy and eventual commitment. And, after all is said and done, that, quite simply, is what a Synagogue is all about.

But, the awareness has not yet come to enough places. Too many Synagogues are still empty because too many Rabbis and Synagogue leaders still do not understand what Jews really want or need.

In this fast-paced, confusing world, each one of us needs structure and direction, a sense of identity and belonging. We seek answers to the age-old questions of existence, and, at the very same time, we need help in confronting brand-new challenges. We want to find God and approach Him with our longings, needs, hopes and fears, and we need to do it both with a sense of authentic tradition *and* with familiar idiom; with words, symbols and music that accurately express our own problems, passions and possibilities.

The Synagogue can still be the place that we do all these things. But, at a time when so many Jews no longer feel compelled to *daven* three times a day, the Synagogue must offer reason to come and satisfaction at being there.

It may mean hurt feelings and bruised egos, it may mean that old forms must be thrown away and new configurations created out of the void, but we *can* bring joy and happiness, intellectual fulfillment and emotional satisfaction back to the Synagogue.

If you are willing to struggle and work, you can make the Synagogue into the place you want it and expect it to be: the place where you seek God and find Him, where you sing His songs and learn His word, where you hug and love and care for each other.

The Synagogue needs you and you need it. Instead of abandoning it, join in fixing it. Make the Synagogue listen to you, respond to your needs and reflect your desires. Then, you, and the hundreds of thousands of Jews like you, can comfortably and joyfully come home again.

LEARNING

To make Jewish education exciting and attractive at all levels and for all age groups, new realities must be recognized and sweeping changes need to be made.

HEBREW SCHOOLS

Even with all their inherent problems—lack of time; tired, unmotivated students; untrained, underpaid teachers and lack of parental support—Hebrew Schools *can* provide basic Jewish education in a positive setting.

To do so, Hebrew Schools cannot operate on faith like an old *shtiebel*, on fear like an old *cheder* or by chance like most contemporary Congregational Schools. Instead, Hebrew Schools must learn the best in secular educational theories, practices and methodologies and apply them to the specific situation of a part-time religious school setting.

The first thing that parents, children and educators must know is what Hebrew Schools *cannot do*. Hebrew

Schools cannot be the place where a child will learn to read, write and speak Hebrew; to *daven* a complete Service; to know the Bible, to translate *Chumash* with Rashi; to have a grasp of every period of Jewish history; to become an ardent Zionist; to properly celebrate Holidays and Festivals; to translate Jewish values into social action and to appreciate the beauty of Jewish culture and customs—all in six hours a week.

Yet, most Jewish educators would like to be able to teach all these subjects and skills and most Jewish parents expect Hebrew Schools to convey the breadth and depth of Jewish knowledge. So, Hebrew Schools still try to teach everything. But, it is an impossible task because there are too many subjects and too little time. That is why Jewish education in America has been justly accused of being "a mile wide and an inch deep." Expectations go unmet, educators are frustrated, parents are disappointed and, worst, children learn very little.

So, the very first thing that each and every Hebrew School must do is *define its goals*. Every legitimate, successful educational institution can clearly state its reasons for being and its educational goals, and, then, articulate its educational philosophy. A Hebrew School can be no different. Every Rabbi, every Jewish Educator, every Jewish parent who sits on a School Board or an Education Committee must decide: "recognizing the limitations of structure and given the limitations of time, what do I want my Hebrew School to accomplish?"

Every community, every Synagogue, every Rabbi and Educator, every parent group may have differing goals and varying priorities. Some will want to produce students who can speak modern Hebrew fluently. Some will concentrate on Bible studies. Others will stress prayer and Synagogue skills. Still others will emphasize history or Zionism or Jewish culture.

There are no right or wrong answers, no right or wrong choices, and so it will be painful to limit areas of instruction, to eliminate subjects which must be taught.

But, rather than trying to teach everything and failing, it is much better for Hebrew Schools to teach a few subjects thoroughly and well. As difficult as it will be, each Hebrew School must make its choices so that any parent can come and ask, "what is the goal of your Hebrew School, what will my child learn here?" and get a concise, straight answer.

Once the goal is articulated and the subject choices are made, then Hebrew Schools must create a course-by-course, subject-by-subject curriculum, based on a scope and sequence of basic skills.

Educational theory teaches that knowledge is acquired by building skills, one upon the other, in a sequential pattern. A subject matter to be taught is broken down into its component parts and learned, part by part, until, eventually, the whole is known. If English reading can be taught this way, so can Hebrew reading; if world history can be taught this way, so can Jewish history.

Hebrew Schools must understand this educational principle and fashion the curriculum to reflect it. Then, they must adopt an *individualized* approach to Jewish learning.

Currently, most Hebrew Schools group children in large, often overcrowded, grade level classroom settings. An entire class is taught the same subject at the same time and the class devolves to the lowest common denominator: the slowest student sets the pace. But, each child is a unique human being with special needs, talents, strengths and weaknesses. So, by using a scope and sequence of skills, a Hebrew School can offer individualized instruction—lessons tailored to the ability and the evolving achievement of each student.

Each subject is "packaged" into small achievement units. Each unit has a stated goal and a performance measurement. Taught, supervised and encouraged by the teacher, each student works at his own pace. When one unit is finished, achievement is measured and recognition is given. Then, a building block of learning is in place and the next unit is begun. With this method, each student knows what is expected, works towards his individual goals, feels a sense of accomplishment and continually acquires more and more knowledge.

This individualized approach to learning helps solve many of the problems which have continually plagued Hebrew Schools:

First, it permits a more flexible, less rigid scheduling. If a student misses a class because of Little League or ballet, the lesson can be made up at another time, in a different setting. The measure of the success of a Hebrew School is not how often a child puts his *"tush"* in a classroom chair, but how much he, ultimately, learns.

Secondly, there is a clear measure of performance and, thus, academic accountability. The curriculum is set. It is not dependent on the whim of a teacher or the chance that a text might not be finished by the end of a school year. What and how much must be learned is stated from the very beginning. So, expectations are clear and whether or not they are met is easily determined.

Finally, the onus and responsibility of learning is put back where it belongs—on the student and, by extension, the parents. So many students come to Hebrew Schools today from homes that have little, if any, Jewish observance, and from parents who may not know how to recite a blessing or read a sentence of Hebrew. They are resentful of the time that is taken from their busy lives and their attitude says, "I *dare you* to teach me anything." And Hebrew Schools, committed to Jewish life and learning, make valiant attempts to reach these children, but, against such odds, are doomed to failure.

Yet, instead of reconciling themselves to the attitudes brought by students and parents, Hebrew Schools have every right to say, "Yes, it is our responsibility to teach. But, it is equally your responsibility to learn. This will be a serious academic institution and, if you want the reward at the end (graduation; candidacy for Bar/Bat Mitzvah) then, just as at any other school, you must meet our standards and requirements. You will not pass from

grade to grade and assume that you will have a Bar/Bat
Mitzvah as a natural right, simply by showing up year
after year. You must do the work and demonstrate your
achievements."

When Hebrew Schools begin to take themselves seriously, the students and their parents will have no choice
but to treat Hebrew Schools with the respect they deserve.

But, no matter how clear the goals, no matter how
well crafted the curriculum, no matter how defined the
educational philosophy or how serious the standards,
Hebrew Schools, ultimately, succeed or fail through the
teachers who are in the classrooms.

Hebrew School teachers, first, must be *educators*.
Educators are not just people with knowledge about a
subject, who stand in front of a classroom, somehow
conveying what they know to others. A mathematician is
not, necessarily a mathematics teacher; a speaker of
English is not, necessarily an English teacher. Nor is a
college student who went to Camp Ramah a Jewish
history teacher or an Israeli, a Hebrew teacher. Teachers—educators—are highly skilled professionals who have
studied educational theory, curriculum development,
pedagogy, classroom management, child psychology, motivation and discipline. Public schools demand teachers
who have a mastery of a particular subject *and* formal
training in education. Hebrew Schools can demand no
less.

Secondly, Hebrew Schools must find *specialists*
rather than generalists. At an elementary level, public
schools have generalists, teachers who teach all subjects
in a contained classroom. But, as courses become more
advanced, subjects more specialized, public schools depend on experts in a particular field. A superb math
teacher is not required to be an expert in English Literature. So, Hebrew Schools need to have faculties of specialists. An outstanding Hebrew language teacher need

not teach Jewish history. A fine social studies teacher need not know the intricacies of Hebrew grammar. Hebrew Schools will take a giant step toward improvement when they permit teachers to concentrate in their specific field of expertise, rather than forcing them to instruct in every subject.

At the same time, Hebrew Schools need to take advantage of the skills, knowledge and expertise of members of the community. Parents, members of the Congregation, Jews and non-Jews in the community are hidden, but incredibly valuable sources of information. In addition to the usual "technique" of inviting guest speakers to class, mini-courses, short seminars and one or two day sessions can be developed around people who bring their special awareness and talents to Jewish education. An attorney can teach the similarities and differences between Jewish and American civil law. A doctor can teach about bio-medical ethics from the scientific and the Jewish perspectives. People who lived through now-historical events (immigration to America from an Eastern European *shtetl;* the Holocaust; Israel's War for Independence; the formation of community institutions) can share their personal, intimate experiences. Teachers are everywhere. It takes a good educator to find them, teach them how to teach and bring them into the classroom to transmit their knowledge.

Finally, teachers must be *role models.* If a Hebrew School wants to inspire Jewish observance and Jewish participation, then its teachers must be practicing, observing Jews. A Hebrew School teacher who is at the shopping mall on Saturday morning loses credibility, but a Hebrew School teacher who is seen by his students in Shul on Shabbat morning proves that he lives what he teaches.

And, Hebrew School teachers cannot continue to reinforce their reputations as foreboding, strict, rigid disciplinarians. Hebrew School teachers must be warm, caring, loving human beings who love their Judaism and who love their students. A smile, a personal word, a hug, *menschlichkite, rachmonos* and love all belong in Hebrew School classrooms and the right teachers put them there.

So, where do we find people like this—teachers who are at the same time trained educators, specialists in their fields, committed Jews and loving role models? Except in a few large cities, very few people like this exist. And, even in the large cities, there are hardly enough of them to go around.

There is only one choice. If the kind of Hebrew School teachers we want and need are not available, then new people must be sought out and trained. Every Jewish community, of every size, must have an intensive Teacher Training Program, sponsored by its Bureau of Jewish Education, by a coalition of Synagogues or, even by one Congregation, in cooperation, if at all possible, with a local college or university. A course of study to train Hebrew School teachers should include the principles of educational theory and practice, and specific subjects that are taught in Hebrew Schools: Hebrew language, Jewish history, Prayer and Synagogue skills, Bible and more.

In this way, a trained educator can be taught the material to convey Jewish subjects. Someone with a background in Judaica can gain skills in pedagogy. A person with little or no Jewish education and no training as an educator can learn both.

Thus, a community can take its own people—whose only requirements are time and interest—and develop a corps of well-trained, qualified, committed Hebrew School teachers. It will benefit Hebrew Schools immeasurably and, undoubtedly, bring new creativity and satisfaction to the lives of many, many people.

In order for Hebrew Schools to attract really fine teachers, they must begin to pay decent salaries. Many Hebrew School teachers have left the profession in recent years because salaries are so low. Young people, who are considering a career in Jewish education, are put off by the low potential income. Part-time teachers and the people who will participate in the Teacher Training Program want to be paid properly. They want to know that their talents, skills and dedication are appreciated and they want to be justly compensated for their work.

No one becomes a Hebrew School teacher to get rich, but everyone is entitled to be paid a living wage, commensurate with training and experience. Hebrew Schools must provide fair remuneration and economic incentive, so that professional dignity and financial security become not only the right but the reality for every teacher.

Finally, in order to make Hebrew Schools relevant and exciting to their students, the most modern techniques and technologies must be used.

Until only ten or fifteen years ago, the textbooks that were available for Hebrew Schools were no different from the books that had been used fifty years before. Most were dull and dreary, offering little stimulation to young minds.

Fortunately, a few publishers—most notably Behrman House, Alternatives in Religious Education and the Union of American Hebrew Congregations—have begun to produce new texts which are educationally sound and aesthetically pleasing. They reflect an understanding of the process of child development, educational sequencing and an awareness of the students' concurrent secular studies.

We now have available Hebrew language texts which are clear as to approach: phonetic or whole word method; Biblical or modern conversational Hebrew. They understand that a grammatical principle can rarely be introduced in Hebrew if the student has not yet learned that principle in his native language—English. History texts are coordinated with what children are learning in their secular studies. Theology is explained to ten year olds, and Holidays and life-cycle events are systematized into cogent units of study. Jewish ethics are articulated, and students are challenged to express feelings and clarify values.

As additional textbooks are created and developed, it must be remembered that Hebrew School books succeed as learning tools for this generation of young people if, and only if, they effectively translate ancient truths into modern idiom, all the while recognizing sound educational principles and respecting the divergence of ability, background and commitment which each student brings to his studies.

New texts have made an important contribution toward improving the quality of Hebrew Schools, but what they have done so far is only a beginning.

For, even the best texts are not enough, because children no longer learn from books alone. And, it is no longer even enough to have a drawer full of film strips and rent an occasional 16 mm. movie. Hebrew Schools must have and use the most up-to-date audio and video equipment and computers.

Every Hebrew School must have a television set and a VCR to utilize the many video tapes that are now available on a wide variety of Jewish subjects. Hebrew language vibrates on a Hebrew Sesame Street-like program. Historical moments come alive with tapes like *Masada* and *Fiddler on the Roof,* the television mini-series *Golda* and the docu-drama *Holocaust.* In addition, Hebrew Schools must own a video camera so that students can create their own video tapes.

One Hebrew School, recently, had the children record video histories with elderly Jews who were interviewed by the students about their life experiences. To prepare for the interviews, and in order to ask sensible questions, the children had to learn about a certain historical period and the specific Jewish events which took place at that time. They came to understand that history is not just in books, but in the people around them and in themselves. And, they know that when the elderly Jews whom they interviewed eventually die, their stories will not die, because they are permanently inscribed on video tape for later generations to see, hear and learn.

Another Hebrew School had the children develop a "You Were There" series with major Jewish historical figures. The students researched the time and place in which a person had lived, the architecture, food and dress of the period and the person's accomplishments and contributions to Jewish life. They wrote the scripts, cast the parts, found the wardrobes, built the sets and directed the tapings. The young man who played Rashi and the young woman who was Henrietta Szold know and will remember more about those characters than any textbook could ever teach. And the students who see those video productions in the years to come will learn more in twenty minutes of video viewing than in hours of reading or lectures.

In addition, every Hebrew School must have computers. The Institute for Computers in Jewish Life in Chicago has already developed dozens of disks. One disk takes the children on a trip to Israel, simulating the airplane, the check through customs and the bus trips to the cities, *kibbutzim* and historical sites. The computer has the student bargain for merchandise in the *shuk* and write a note to God to be placed in the Western Wall. Another disk is called "Brachot Boxes." A student is asked to identify which blessing is to be recited over a specific kind of food and, if correct, is permitted to place an "X" or "O" in a tic-tac-toe game played against the computer. "Jewish I.Q. Baseball" asks questions of general Jewish knowledge and a correct answer is rewarded with a single, double, triple, or home run on the simulated baseball diamond. Many other equally interesting and exciting disks give children the opportunity to approach Jewish learning through the modern instrumentality of the computer.

Our children use computers at secular schools and at home to enhance their learning and to have fun while gaining new knowledge. There is no reason that Hebrew Schools should not take advantage of the same technology.

The result? When was the last time you heard of a child unwilling to leave Hebrew School?

Just the other day, a father who had come to pick up his son at Hebrew School was told: "I can't leave yet, Dad."

"Why not?" asked the father, "it's time to go."

"I can't leave yet, Dad. It's my turn next on the computer."

It will take a great deal of money to write new curricula, develop Teacher Training Programs, pay teachers what they deserve, publish new texts, buy video and computer hardware and create new video tapes and computer disks. Already, most Hebrew Schools are subsidized between 30% and 60% by their Synagogues' budgets, because tuition cannot possibly cover all the expenses.

But, what better, more important way is there to spend Jewish money than on educating our children? Synagogues will have to spend larger percentages of their budgets and Federations will have to provide the communities' financial assistance. But, we have no choice. For, we must spend Jewish money now, to teach our children the richness of their past, in order to insure the creative viability of their future.

Hebrew Schools *can* be infused with new direction, new quality and new spirit so that they can have renewed success in touching Jewish children's minds and hearts. Let's not give up on our Hebrew Schools, but, let's commit the energy and the resources to make them into the places our children deserve and from which they will emerge educated and inspired.

DAY SCHOOLS

The real answer to high quality, intensive Jewish education is Jewish Day Schools.

Since shortly after World War II, Jewish communities throughout the United States have established Orthodox Jewish Day Schools. In the last thirty years, Conservative, Community and, now, Reform Day Schools have grown up.

Depending on denominational orientation, Day Schools will differ in religious philosophy, level of religious observance, time spent on various subjects and requirements for teaching staff. But, whatever the specific perspective, most all Jewish Day Schools have much in common, because a Jewish Day School has so many things "going for it" that it is bound to provide a much more thorough, in-depth Jewish education than an afternoon Hebrew School can possibly give.

A Jewish Day School, first, has *time*. Because of the amount of time available, a Jewish Day School does not have to choose subjects to be taught, but can introduce children to the entire range of Jewish learning: Hebrew reading, writing, speaking and literature; Bible; sacred texts; history; Holidays; prayers and Synagogue skills; customs and ceremonies; theology and philosophy; Israel, Zionism, local and world Jewry; *tzedakah,* ethics and values. There is no need for hard choices, no need to eliminate any subject. A Day School can teach everything.

A Jewish Day School has a *seriousness of purpose*. Because Judaic Studies is an "academic subject," just like math or science, it is seen and treated by the students with the seriousness it deserves.

A Jewish Day School attracts *excellent teachers*. Because a Jewish Day School can offer full-time employment, at a salary fairly comparable to local public schools, high quality teachers are willing and eager to be part of the faculty. In addition, because of state licensing and certification requirements, most all Day School teachers must be trained educators, as well as specific subject experts. Finally, because of its special nature, most teachers who choose to be part of a Jewish Day School staff, are committed to Jewish lifestyle and rituals, making them excellent role models for their students.

A Jewish Day School has *parental support*. It takes a special kind of commitment and a significant financial investment to send a child to a Jewish Day School. Parents who choose a Jewish Day School for children are going to be interested and involved in the educational process and support their childrens' programs and assignments. It is true that not *every* parent sends his child to a Jewish Day School for the Jewish education it gives or the Jewish interest it implies. Some children come because parents are seeking a good private school, or because the Day School offers extended daycare, or because the School is close to home. But, the Talmud teaches that even though someone does something, originally, for an ulterior motive, he may, eventually, come to do it for its own sake. A Jewish parent who cares enough to send his child to a Jewish Day School, whatever the original reason, knows what will take place at the School and supports it. And, every Jewish child who comes to a Jewish Day School means that one more person is exposed to the world of Jewish learning.

At a Jewish Day School, Judaism is a *normal part of life*. For children who attend a Jewish Day School, Hebrew and Judaic Studies do not have to be "pigeon-holed" in their minds, relegated to "a couple of hours, a couple of afternoons a week." They are, instead, life experiences. At a Jewish Day School, Hebrew is a living language, read and spoken naturally, in a bilingual setting. Jewish history is learned in context so that historical events need not be separated into "regular" and "Jewish," but are understood as they happened, as one historical whole. A Jewish "uniform," a *kepa*, is worn during Judaic Studies, meals and Services, and, later, a *tallis* and *tephillin* are added to the "uniform." Proper blessings are recited with meals and children participate in *tefilot*, prayer Services, which are both learning experiences and the opportunity to *daven*, to know and worship God. Children become comfortable and "at home" in a Synagogue and with a

Prayerbook. The calendar of the Day School revolves around the calendar and the rhythms of Jewish life.

Jewish Day School students form warm and close relationships with their classmates and other students in the School, which are often strong and lasting.

And, because Jewish Day School students do not need to attend an afternoon Hebrew School, they are free every afternoon to play with friends in the neighborhood, to play Little League and soccer, to take music, dance and other lessons, to join Scouts and to do school homework early in the day.

Thus, a Jewish Day School student has two sets of friends, two places to develop and have relationships and enough time to participate in extra-curricular activities.

A Jewish Day School shows children, in word and in deed, that being Jewish is a way of life and that participation in Jewish observances and rituals can be normal, everyday experiences, without at all jeopardizing involvement in the rest of the world.

A Jewish Day School teaches Jewish *values*. In addition to teaching Hebrew, Bible and history, a Jewish Day School is a place where Jewish ethics and values are lived and taught. A Jewish Day School helps create children who are steeped in Jewish priorities and choices. In order to face the "real world" out there, children need a firm and resolute sense of self. They must know who they are and for what they stand. A Jewish Day School gives a child a sense of identity and authenticity; a sense that he is part of a People that has been guided, for millenia, by a standard of ethics and behavior which has transcended time, place and situation.

Jewish Day Schools are well aware of all the arguments about pluralism, universalism and egalitarianism, and the case made for supporting public education. But, what kind of value system, for our children, is coming out of America today, and from public schools, specifically? Public schools cannot teach a moral system that derives from any particular faith community, because, by definition, public schools must be amoral. So, if morality and

ethics are discussed in a public school setting, it is either
as a philosophical academic exercise, the personal opinion of a teacher foisted on a class, or amongst the youngsters on the playground. Yet, we live in a world of
dizzying and confounding choices. Our children are challenged and tempted everywhere they turn, and public
schools offer no answers.

But, in a Jewish Day School, *menschlichkite* is both a
guide and a goal. A Jewish Day School imparts the
eternal and enduring truths of Judaism as they relate to
today's world and life's challenges, and, at the same time,
is guided by Judaism's call for justice, righteousness,
compassion and kindness. Students are taught to be
human and humane; how to behave toward each other in
work and at play, in joy and in anger. A Jewish Day
School has the time and the sensitive staff to respond,
immediately, with care, concern and guidance, to the
little and big crises of everyday life and to the sometimes
difficult task of growing up.

Jewish children deserve to be exposed to and immersed in Jewish ethics and values, and a Jewish Day
School does just that.

A modern Jewish Day School does not have to be an
old-fashioned Yeshiva which attempts to "indoctrinate"
students toward a specific religious belief system and
demand a certain level of observance. A contemporary
Jewish Day School can present Jewish learning and
observance in the most gentle, non-threatening way,
without teaching ritual absolutes. A Jewish Day School
offers the beauty and the richness of the Jewish heritage—history, tradition, life-enhancing ceremonies—
without judgments or pressures. What a child and a
family do with the knowledge is up to them.

But, there is one thing which a Jewish Day School
must do, without question, without debate. A Jewish Day
School must offer a secular education which is as good or
better than the best public or other private school a child
could attend. No Jewish child should sacrifice his secular

education for the sake of a Jewish Day School education. So, Jewish Day School secular studies must be outstanding.

The concept and methodology of *individualized* education must be used so that each child learns to the heights of his own potential. The very best teachers—talented, creative transmitters—must be with children every day, every year. All subjects must be offered, including music, art and physical education, and, in the upper grades, foreign language, lab science, advanced math and literature courses. Enrichment activities must be offered and the facility must include full play areas and sports fields, laboratories and computer centers. A Jewish Day School must go beyond expected school subjects to teach children to study, research and to think—precious, vital skills that will be with them for a lifetime.

It will cost a great deal of money to organize and maintain high quality Jewish Day Schools, because facilities, equipment and good teachers are expensive. Yet, if it is administered correctly, a Jewish Day School should be able to pay all its own costs, if every student pays full tuition. The problem is that not every family can afford the high tuition costs, and no Jewish child should be denied this kind of intensive Jewish education just because his parents do not have the money. So, Synagogues and Federations will have to provide scholarships for youngsters to attend Jewish Day Schools. As with Hebrew Schools, this will put a new, additional burden on funding organizations, but it must be done.

Fortunately, every American community which has a population of 7,500 or more Jews has at least one Jewish Day School. So many Jewish Day Schools have been established because it is recognized that, while there are no guarantees, a Jewish child who attends a Jewish Day School and is steeped in Jewish learning and observance, has a much better chance of being a knowledgeable, committed, participating Jewish adult. Jewish Day Schools have the great and, already unfolding, potential of creating an entire generation of young American Jews who know Bible, sacred texts and Jewish history, who know how to *daven* and are comfortable in the Synagogue, and who will be active, supporting members of the Jewish community.

Jewish Day Schools deserve the moral and financial support of the community because of the tremendous contribution they make to Jewish life. And, Jewish Day Schools deserve the serious consideration of every Jewish parent as the place to send Jewish children to receive outstanding secular education and in-depth Jewish education in a nurturing atmosphere. For today's Jewish Day Schools will educate and inspire the Jewish leaders of tomorrow.

ADULT EDUCATION

There are a number of reasons why so many Jewish adults do not learn about Judaism or study Jewish subjects.

First, people are busy with their own jobs or professions, with their family and friends and with their own special interests and hobbies. Secondly, the way most classes are arranged means making a fairly long commitment to a time and place. Thirdly, other things which compete for a contemporary Jew's time and effort seem more appealing and attractive. Finally, and, perhaps, most significantly, Jews who are leaders in business, or highly educated practicing professionals, or who have great responsibility for large sums of money, are embarrassed to admit that they cannot read a sentence of Hebrew and know little about Jewish history, rituals or lifestyle. Rather than expose their lack of knowledge, they stay away.

To involve more Jews in Jewish education, Rabbis, Educators and schools must seek new formats and new ways of reaching people.

The Synagogue, itself, must always be, as it was originally intended, a classroom. Whenever a Jew comes to Shul, for whatever reason—every week, occasionally for a Bar Mitzvah, once a year for the High Holidays—he should be able to learn something. The pulpit is not the place for the Rabbi to give political analysis or book reviews, but to teach. A word, a comment, an interpretation, an explanation can enlighten and inform.

Some Congregations set aside one Service a month to be a Teaching Service or a Learner's Minyan. As the Service progresses, its structures and themes are taught; as the prayers are recited, their meaning and interpretations are given. To someone who does not know, the Service can be intimidating and confusing, but a few words of explanation can open the world of Jewish prayer.

Many Synagogues use Torah Reading time for teaching, with questions and answers. Instead of reading the entire lengthy portion, which many do not understand, the weekly *sedra* is discussed and its ideas debated. Other Synagogues ask members to prepare a *d'var Torah* or a *drash*, a Torah lesson, to present. For from out of the responsibility to teach comes real learning.

Just by listening, anyone who sits in a Synagogue can learn in the most "painless" way possible.

Classes that go on week after week, for a semester or more, often suffer from diminished attendance and participation, because interest and enthusiasm cannot be sustained for such a long period of time. To enhance success, classes can be held for no more than four or six weeks (or sessions) at a time. These "mini-classes" require only a short time commitment, so conflicts with other activities are minimized. Expectations are clearly defined, enthusiasm and interest remain high, new knowledge is quickly acquired and the student feels a sense of accomplishment and immediate gratification.

Scheduling of classes must be flexible enough to meet the needs of very busy people. The Synagogue that offers

its Adult Education Program only on Tuesday evening
from 8 p.m. to 10 p.m. in the School Wing of the
Synagogue automatically eliminates everyone who cannot be there then. But, the Synagogue which offers
classes at a variety of times, on a number of days of the
week and in different places, opens the world of Jewish
learning to more people.

Some will prefer weekday morning classes; others,
evening sessions. Carpool driving parents may want a
class offered during the times their children are in Hebrew
School. Businesspeople may respond to an early morning or a lunch-time seminar in a downtown office. Young
couples may want a Saturday or a Sunday evening discussion group in alternating homes, to add a social component and to save money on babysitters. A large apartment building or a condominium complex, in which
many seniors live, may be the perfect setting for a class,
particularly during the cold winter months. The possible
combinations of time and place are infinite, so the more
choice, the more who will come to learn.

Even a three or four week class may be too long, or too
threatening, for some. So, individual class sessions may
appeal. Some Synagogues have a once or twice a month
Sunday morning breakfast program, complete with lox
and bagels, to present guest speakers/teachers on subjects of current interest or controversy. A guest speaker
series, held three or four evenings during the year, or a
visiting scholar-in-residence weekend may attract people,
based either on the popularity of the speaker or interest in
the topic.

There is one class, however, that meets week after
week, which has been consistently successful and popular
at Congregations throughout the country. The Adult
Bar/Bat Mitzvah Program provides an opportunity to
those who have never had a Bar or Bat Mitzvah to prepare
for and participate in this most meaningful ceremony.

The adult students learn to read Hebrew and recite
prayers and blessings. An introduction to Jewish ideas

and concepts—history, literature, theology, Holidays and Synagogue skills—is given to provide a foundation of basic Jewish knowledge. The specific skills necessary for the Bar/Bat Mitzvah ceremony—*trup*, blessings, Haftorah chants—are taught.

Because the motivation to have the Bar/Bat Mitzvah is high, participants in the class willingly invest time and intensity in their studies. They support each other's efforts with high energy and growing excitement. They know that their work has a specific goal, which is clearly attainable and which will be met within an exact period of time.

At the actual Bar/Bat Mitzvah ceremony, each person leads a part of the Service and is called to the Torah. Other parts of the Service are recited together by the group. The speeches, articulating feelings and sentiments, are always full of expressions of accomplishment, joy and love. The moment is charged with high emotion, deep pleasure and satisfaction for the participants, their families and the entire Congregation.

The Adult Bar/Bat Mitzvah is an adult education program that works, because it responds to long held, deeply felt needs, and because it meets the exact goal of adult education—to convey information and create connection with past and future.

The classroom and the lecture hall are not the only places to learn. A camp weekend, in a popular recreational area, may provide the setting to attract people to a short-term learning experience. Film, music, drama, dance, art and museum exhibitions can be pleasant, exciting ways to acquire information.

One Congregation, in the New York area, sponsors an annual one day "Torah-thon," a veritable "supermarket" of hour-long courses, exhibitions and "hands-on" opportunities to do and create. This Torah-thon combines learning with food and fun and has become, as well, a major social event, attracting large crowds.

It is true that "one shot" lectures, films and exhibitions do not have the same educational benefit as a semester's classes, but each program, each session, is valuable in its own way, and every exposure to Jewish knowledge means potential for learning and growth.

The educational "rules" for adults can be no different than for children. Stimulating, effective, exciting teachers must be found. The most modern educational techniques and technologies must be used. A dull lecture, presented by an ill-prepared teacher, can be more harmful for an adult student than for a child, because the adult can get up and leave, never to return.

Textbooks created specifically for adult education must be developed. Until only a few years ago, there was not a decent Hebrew primer for adults. Anyone who wanted to learn beginning Hebrew had to use a text written for an eight year old. It was not only ineffective, but it was embarrassing for a parent and a child to be doing homework out of the same book. Fortunately, this problem has been solved with the publication of a Hebrew primer written especially for adults. Texts for other subjects are needed. Children's books are too simplistic, and yet, regular books may be too advanced for a beginning student.

Course subjects must be interesting and relevant. Too many teachers announce courses in the area of their specialization, disregarding the needs of the learner. Course offerings must be packaged well and marketed cleverly to attract people whose time and energy are being beckoned from every direction. Competition from so many other sources should not mean that Jewish educators "fold their tents" and slink off in defeat, but, rather, rise to the challenge of presenting what Judaism has to offer in exciting, stimulating ways.

Finally, success in adult Jewish education cannot be measured in thousands or even hundreds, but must be numbered by tens and by ones. A teacher is flattered by a class of seventy, but may be able to give more personal attention, more in-depth instruction to ten. From those ten, "turned-on" and enthusiastic students, will come another ten, because successful, satisfied students are the best advertisement for Jewish education. Each student can be asked to bring one more the next time. One by one, ten by ten, Jewish education, in a particular community, can become the popular, fashionable thing to do, the place to be. All it takes is the right approach.

No matter how interesting the subject, how flexible the schedule, how intriguing the setting, there are Jews who, simply, will not take the time, make the effort or have the desire to come and learn. Most Synagogues and educational institutions say, "Well, we tried, we offered the best, the most tantalizing opportunities we could, but if they won't come, there is nothing we can do." Wrong. For, if Jews won't come to Jewish learning, then Jewish learning *must be brought to them*.

Each week, I sent, by first class mail, to every member of my Congregation, a two or three page lesson which is called "Torah Talk." Torah Talk contains a short summary of the weekly Torah Portion and an explanation, comment or interpretation of a sentence or an idea in the Portion. Sometimes a law is discussed; sometimes a *mitzvah* is explained; sometimes an historical moment is explored. The personalities and motivations of the Biblical heroes are examined; modern situations are seen in the light of ancient law; Torah's ethical mandate is presented. Often, a question to be discussed with the children is asked.

It takes no special effort to get Torah Talk. No one has to purchase a thick book, come to a special place or set aside a special time. Torah Talk comes in the mail, directly into people's homes. It takes no more than ten minutes a week to read, and I have been told that Torah Talk is read at the kitchen table, in line at the grocery store, under the hair drier at the beauty shop, in the bleachers at a Little League game, out of a briefcase on a commuter train, in the car and in bed. One family uses a magnet to hold Torah Talk to the refrigerator so that each family member will know where to find it. Other families have punched holes in the papers' sides and keep Torah Talk in a notebook.

One woman wrote to me:

> "Torah Talk is a creative, exciting idea that gets to the very heart of the 'Yuppie' dilemma. That is, our generation has heard and 'knows' that the Torah holds truths and beauty of living, however, most of us do not know what it *really* says and will probably never make the time to find out. You have dealt with this problem by bringing the Torah, relevant, easy to understand, directly into our homes."

If they won't come to learn Torah, Torah goes to them. In creating Torah Talk, I said, "Hopefully, by having Torah in your hands, Torah will enter your hearts." From the reaction so far, it seems to be working. Torah Talk, and projects like it, are not the ultimate answer to the problem of adult Jewish education, but they are a start.

We need more "portable" Jewish learning that can go directly into the homes of people who will not come out to get it. How about computer disks for adult use on home computers? On the simplest level, there can be recipes for Holiday foods and chicken soup. There can be time-lines of Jewish history, outlines of the structure of the Prayerbook, and games, which use, as settings, Jewish historical events.

And, we need video tapes for use on VCR's in Jewish homes. There can be a step-by-step guide to make a Shabbat table or a Pesach Seder. There can be adult versions of "You Were There" with heroes of Jewish history. There can be travel guides to Israel, to Eastern Europe, to places of Jewish interest throughout the world. American Jews can meet Jews from England, from Argentina, from the Soviet Union by video. There can be video tapes of Jewish music and dance, visits to museums and exploration of sites of archeological discoveries.

These "passive" home learning tools—computer disks and video tapes—can be of great benefit, also, for those Jews who will *never* take a class or hear a Rabbi teach because they are among the 70% of American Jews who do not belong to a Synagogue. Yet, someone who "wouldn't set foot" in a Synagogue may be a musician who would be intrigued by a video tape of the history of Jewish music, or an architect who would be fascinated by a video journey to Synagogue buildings throughout the world. Watching one video tape does not a knowledgeable Jew make, but one video tape is one more than none. And every moment of Jewish learning is valid and worthwhile. And, who knows where it may lead?

Shakespeare said that "all the world's a stage." For the modern Jew, every place, using every possible technique, must be a classroom. If we are willing to take risks, to try the untried, to be open to new possibilities, then there is a chance that we can combat Jewish ignorance and convey, once again, the beauty, the intellectual brilliance and the common sense which Judaism teaches. The People of the Book have to find new ways to open the book so that we can know what is inside.

SPECIAL PEOPLE WITH SPECIAL NEEDS

If the Synagogue is to have any place in the lives of today's Jews, then it must understand their individual and special status, needs and hopes. The Synagogue must hear pain and help to ease it; confront confusion and help to lessen it; feel loneliness and help to soften it. To be effective and to fulfill its real purpose, the Synagogue must recognize and respond to the uniqueness of each human being.

• The Synagogue must respond to the changing definition of *family*.

In the 1950's and early 60's, most Jewish families fit
the "traditional" pattern of a working father, a
housewife/mother, two or three kids, a suburban drive-
way with two cars and a basketball hoop over the garage.
We were the living embodiment of "Ozzie and Harriet"
and "Leave it to Beaver," and Synagogue programming
was geared to this configuration. But, now, with so many
single parent families, blended families, non-custodial
parents and "his, hers and our" children, the Synagogue
must be sensitive to new needs.

Simple things first. The time of the Men's Club
"Father-Son Sports Banquet" is over. First, it excludes
the daughters, but, more importantly, too many children
are left out because they do not have fathers in their
everyday lives.
Hebrew School registration forms have to have a place
for two surnames—the child's and the mother's new
married name. The Hebrew School has to know with
which parent the child lives, who is to be called in an
emergency, what information is to be given to which
parent. A child may have step-siblings with whom he
lives who have different last names. The Hebrew School
must know what questions to ask and not be embarrassed
by the answers.
Hebrew School schedules need to be flexible. There
has to be an answer to the father who says, "My children
cannot come to Sunday School, because I get only 48
hours of Court-ordered visitation every two weeks and I
am just not willing to give up those Sunday morning
hours with my kids."

The Synagogue needs support groups for newly divorced people, to help them with the pain, the hurts and
the transition to single life. Divorced, non-custodial parents need a place to talk about the separation and the

loneliness they experience, and to find new friends with whom to share holidays and other former-family times.

Single parents need to know that they are not alone. There are others who share their situation and face some of their unique challenges. A Synagogue sponsored support group will bring these people together to meet, talk, to find new friends, to solve similar problems—even something as simple as Hebrew School car pools for working mothers. And, frankly, a group of this kind will permit single parents to get away from the constant responsibility of the children for an hour or three and have a real, adult conversation. And, if a single parent mother happens to meet a single parent father, and a date or two results, or the two families join together for an outing or a holiday celebration, so much the better.

At Bar and Bat Mitzvah and other celebrations, the Synagogue and, particularly, the Rabbi must be ready to accept and sensitively deal with a multitude of family configurations. A child may have four parents, multiple sets of grandparents and brothers and sisters with two or three different last names. Deeply involved in a child's life may be Mommy's boyfriend or Daddy's live-in lover. The Synagogue should offer the respect and honor which everyone deserves, but, at times, it must be ready to be the arbiter between warring ex-spouses with hurt feelings and leftover angers. Sometimes, the Synagogue is the only real advocate that the *child* has at his own Bar Mitzvah. It is a new and different role that the Synagogue must play.

All Synagogue programs must be aware of the new status of families. Instead of two parents and two children, Synagogue events may be filled with large, extended families, including grandparents, assorted cousins, close neighbors and "significant others." Or, a mother and a child may be alone, without any family or friends. Everyone must be welcomed and accepted for whom and what he is without any preconceived expectations or judgments. The Synagogue must become the "superstructure" of family and community into which everyone fits comfortably and happily.

• The Synagogue must respond to the large number of Jewish *singles*.

Those adults who choose to be single need to have their choice and their lifestyle accepted and respected. There has to be a place and a role for singles in the Synagogue, even though they will not use the Schools, Youth Programs or Couple's Club. Synagogue social activities cannot be exclusively "couple" oriented because too many people will be excluded. Single adults may want and need relationships with young children or a place to celebrate Pesach or Chanukah. The Synagogue can help "match" families, who would love an "honorary" aunt or uncle, with singles, who would be glad to have a six year old to hug once in a while or a teen-ager to take to a ball game.

Someone may walk into the Synagogue alone, but he or she must not be allowed to be lonely. The Synagogue needs to open arms wide to embrace and to meet the needs of singles by choice.

And, if the Synagogue is serious about stemming the number of intermarriages, raising the Jewish birthrate and, truly, meeting human needs, then the Synagogue must help find husbands and wives for Jewish singles who want to be married.

Enough of the loneliness! Enough of the heartbreak! Enough of the singles' bars and the "meat markets!"

Synagogues can run dignified, worthwhile programs for Jewish singles to meet each other. The horrible dances and "mixers" can be replaced by Young Business and Professional Groups, where people come to meet, learn, listen to speakers, view films and engage in discussion and debate, without the pressure of wondering, "who will ask me to dance?"

But, better yet, it's about time that the Synagogue gives God a little help. A Midrash asks, "What has God been doing since He created the world? Answer: He's been matching couples." But, it seems that God may be too busy lately to have time for this old, noble task. So, it's time for us to take over.

Yenta, of *Fiddler on the Roof,* is the prototype *shaddchan,* the matchmaker. It may seem demeaning, it may seem to ignore spontaneity, and, even, love, but, it works!

Let the Rabbi or another Synagogue professional meet, on a personal basis, the singles in the community. The Rabbi gets to know someone and his or her likes, dislikes, needs, wants, and when he knows a certain man who might be right for a certain woman, he makes the match, the introduction.

It is a wonderful role for the Synagogue to play—to bring two people together and watch love be found and grow. It contributes to the happiness of two precious human beings and to the strength of the Jewish people.

• The Synagogue must come to understand the growing community of Jewish *gays.*

What was once a closely guarded secret is now a simple fact of life. There are tens of thousands of gay Jews in America today. In recent years, they have "come out of the closet" to proudly, and sometimes, militantly, proclaim their sexual preferences and to present a new challenge to the Synagogue and the Jewish community.

Frankly, as open and as accepting as many wish to be, the issue of how to respond to gay Jews may take a generation or two to resolve. Many traditional Jews regard homosexuality, as does the Torah, as an "abomination," punishable, if not in Biblical terms of death, then, at least, by denial and rejection. However, the fact is that gays are with us and they are Jews; they are human beings, with feelings, rights and needs. They deserve to be respected for *who they are,* even if they are not accepted, by some, for *what they do.*

The Synagogue need not "celebrate" homosexual lifestyle, nor need it equivocate on Judaism's teachings about the primacy of heterosexual relationships, the sanctity of marriage and the high value placed on having and rearing children.

But, the Synagogue needs to understand that there are Jews who are not interested in getting married; who will not be having Jewish babies; who will not be involved in traditional family programming; who may want to bring a lover to Shul, without the fear of being ostracized; who may want a sense of family, without producing one; who may want to love and hold or even have a child without giving birth to one. These Jews must be welcomed without judgment, but with understanding.

At the same time, the Synagogue must respect gays' choices to form, if they wish, their own Congregations, where they may feel more comfortable with each other. This is not a new or revolutionary idea in Jewish life. When immigrants came from Europe at the end of the 19th and the beginning of the 20th centuries, they often formed Shuls whose membership was strictly from the city or town in the "old country" from which they had come. Various trades—the butchers, the shoemakers, the tanners, the clothiers—had their own Shuls. It took a generation or two for these people to no longer need each other for special support, and to feel accepted enough to fully integrate into other Congregations. It may be the same for Jewish gays today, who are in their first years of "immigration" into contemporary American and Jewish society.

Jewish homosexuals and lesbians cannot be the lepers or the pariahs of the Jewish community. They deserve understanding. And, it will be to their benefit, and to the benefit of the Synagogue, when that understanding is given.

• The Synagogue must respond to the ever-increasing number of *elderly* Jews.

It seems odd to suggest that the Synagogue must have a special sensitivity to the needs of the elderly, because, for generations, it has been the older Jews who have been the mainstay of Synagogue life. The Shul was their realm and domain, and only with smiling forebearance did the "old-timers," the self-styled "A-K's," permit the "youngsters" any say in Shul affairs. But, the "Bubbie and Zayde," whose lives, literally, centered around the Synagogue, whose piety kept the *minyan* full, and whose tenacity kept the kitchen meticulously kosher and gleamingly spotless, have, in great part, been replaced, in our time, by the modern-day "Grandma and Grandpa," who are as likely to be found shopping on Fifth Avenue, speeding to a tennis lesson in a fire engine red sports car or scaling a mountain on a Club Med vacation.

The Synagogue must speak to both Zayde and Grandpa with equal respect and with appropriate activities.

The Synagogue must create, on a more personal, intimate level, the same kind of programs for the elderly that the Federation will do on a community-wide basis.

A group of volunteers within the Synagogue must be available to drive the elderly to Services and other Synagogue activities. Teen-agers can provide strong legs and arms to help with grocery shopping and errands. A phone call a day from a friendly, caring person provides human contact, friendship and the assurance that the homebound senior is feeling well. Doctors in the Congregation can provide low-cost medical care; attorneys, legal advice; and pharmacists, at-cost medications. An Adopt-a-Grandparent Program offers a "ready-made" family for holiday and birthday celebrations, when children and grandchildren are thousands of miles away.

The Synagogue can run programs designed specifically for seniors: a low-cost luncheon program with speakers, films and entertainment; gatherings in various housing complexes and high rise apartment buildings so that seniors need not travel at night or on cold winter days; a widow-to-widow support group to help with grief, loneliness and practical tasks such as banking and investments; a room for card playing, mah-jongg, listening to music, chatting; a host of volunteer programs for the seniors within the Synagogue so that their years of experience and expertise can be put to productive use; dances, social activities, theater groups and more, because life, enjoyment, fun, sexual activity, needing and being needed do not end at 65.

The Synagogue must be ever-ready to help with new situations and problems when they arise. A few years ago, for example, when the United States was going through terrible economic times, a quiet panic set in amongst seniors who had retired to the West Coast from the East and the Midwest. They had been assured that their savings, pensions and social security would mean comfort and dignity in their older years. But, with inflation devastating their dollars, they were afraid that their fixed incomes would no longer provide for their financial security. So, one Synagogue invited all its senior citizens to a series of meetings with financial planners, investment counsellors, bankers and lawyers who offered advice on how to face hard economic times. Not only was the professional advice invaluable, but two dozen seniors, who had been terribly frightened by events which they could not control, knew that they were not alone; others shared their dilemma and fears. That knowledge, that sharing, meant new-found confidence, comfort and healing.

The Yom Kippur prayer, "do not cast me off in my old age," cannot be addressed just to God, but must be heard by the Synagogue, too.

• The Synagogue must be sensitive to the needs and the rights of the *handicapped* and the *disabled*.

Jewish children deserve a Jewish education even when they do not fit the preconceived notion of "bright, beautiful and precocious." There are tens of thousands of Jewish children with learning disabilities—dyslexia, developmental lags, perceptual-motor deficiencies, minimal brain dysfunction—and with physical handicaps.

Their secular schools provide for access, mainstreaming where possible, and special classes when needed. The Jewish schools can do no less. We must open the world of Jewish learning to every young person, by developing curriculum and materials and by training teachers to meet the needs of the mentally and physically disabled.

Happily, a number of programs—for both Hebrew Schools and summer camps—have already been created to fulfill this obligation. But, these programs cannot be isolated in a few privileged places. They must spread across the country so that the heartache of incapacity need not be compounded by the inability of the Synagogue to provide warm understanding and practical help.

Rabbis and educators must know that not every Bar/Bat Mitzvah child will be capable of meeting all the usual expectations. Yet, a meaningful ceremony can be tailored to the talents and abilities of each individual. The pride of his parents and the smile of accomplishment of the youngster who successfully recites the *brachas,* because that reaches the heights of his own capabilities, is worth at least as much as all the Maftirs and Haftorahs of his peers.

At the same time, every Synagogue must be open to every person—child or adult—with physical handicap. There must be wheelchair access to every place within the Synagogue facility—including the *bimah.* There must be large-type Prayerbooks and Bibles for the sight impaired and Braille texts for the blind. There must be sound-enhancing equipment for the hard of hearing and signing for the deaf.

Every Jew deserves equal access to his heritage and to his People, and no mental or physical handicap can be permitted to block the way.

• The Synagogue must be the place where Jewish *teen-agers* can come to find direction and guidance.

It is not easy growing up in America today. New discoveries, based on space-age technologies, wipe out long held assumptions overnight. Travel and communications have made the once large world into a tiny village. An endless variety of choices abound. Drugs and alcohol lure. Sexual activity attracts and sexual diseases threaten. Cults and gurus lurk. The abundance of career choices confuse. The possibility of nuclear destruction hovers. Relationships seek to be defined, maturity needs to be nurtured and love waits to be found.

Who or what is going to help Jewish teen-agers face the questions and find the answers? Parents should and will try, but many young people, growing toward independence, shun parental advice. An occasional teacher may guide or inspire, but that connection depends on chance or luck. Older siblings rarely have time or patience, and peers, equally confused and searching, offer little help.

So the Synagogue can and must be the one place that Jewish teen-agers can find companionship, unconditional acceptance, structure and direction.

Every Synagogue must have a solid, exciting Youth Program, with Youth Groups for children as young as 4th or 5th grade. The Youth Groups, first, give Jewish youngsters a place to meet, to gather and to be with each other, because, if the Synagogue is really interested in promoting Jewish marriages, then young Jews must be able to find each other. It is never too soon, because social and dating patterns are established early, and, as one Rabbi taught, "dating leads to mating." With Jewish teen-agers no longer living in one neighborhood, but spread out over many miles and attending many different high schools, the Synagogue must be the focus, the one central address for being together.

So, the Youth Groups must offer fine social, recreational and cultural activities. There must be a Teen Lounge—with comfortable furniture; a stereo with records and tapes; a soda machine; ping-pong and pool tables; study carrels; books and magazines; a television and a VCR—where teens can simply drop in and "hang out." There need to be athletic facilities, playing fields and sports equipment. There must be parties, dances, weekend activities; speakers, films, discussions; overnight retreats, trips to places of interest, exposure to new ideas, people and things. There must be fun, good times, good friends. There must be testing and trying; developing skills; involvement in group dynamics; opportunities for management and leadership. To help accomplish all this, excellent advisors must be found who will be role models, confidants, teachers, friends.

In addition, the Synagogue must offer religious and educational opportunities on an increasingly mature level. The Synagogue must joyously welcome the teenagers at Services and prove that there is a place for them between Junior Congregation and marriage. Teens who come to Shul must be given *aliyot* on a regular basis, and those who are capable should be invited to lead parts of the *davening*. One Synagogue has teen-agers chant all the High Holiday Torah and Haftorah portions. Over the objections of some Congregants who want the honors for themselves, that Synagogue makes an important statement about its priorities and its future.

When a Synagogue is, for whatever reasons, unwilling or unable to involve teens in the worship, then, a Youth Congregation needs to be established where the young people can conduct their own Services. Charismatic leaders need to be found who will excite, inspire and keep the teens coming and actively participating.

The Synagogue bemoans the fact that so many young people "drop out" of Jewish education after Bar/Bat

Mitzvah. To keep the teen-agers interested and participating, the Synagogue must offer high level educational programs which are worthy of a busy young person's time and energy.

The Synagogue, usually in a cooperation with a local Bureau of Jewish Education, can frequently offer high school level Hebrew language courses, where students get full foreign language credit at their secular high schools.

As teens learn, in their high schools, in an increasingly maturing and sophisticated way, about world history, literature, philosophy and more, they must learn, in the same way, about Jewish history, literature and philosophy. Otherwise, while their secular knowledge grows and expands, they will be left with only the Jewish information they had when they turned thirteen. So, our teen-agers must be given classes and courses which meet their growing need to know, and respect their new academic abilities and intellectual maturity. The classes and teachers cannot be merely dull information conveyors, but must be creative, exciting and challenging.

Further, and perhaps most importantly, discussion seminars need to be conducted on the highest level of maturity and trust. Jewish teen-agers want and need Jewish insights into the challenges that face them. After all those years of Hebrew School, they welcome the chance to translate Jewish values and ethics into everyday situations.

How can Jewish teachings help with relationships with parents, between siblings, with friends? Does Judaism have anything to say about drug and substance use? How does Judaism help make choices about sexual activity? Does the Synagogue have any place in helping to avoid drunk driving? Why is Judaism so opposed to intermarriage? What difference does it make what religion someone is? Can Judaism help with political choices? toward ending world hunger? with issues of war and peace and nuclear disarmament? What does Judaism have to say about all the questions of bio-medical ethics: test-tube babies? birth control? euthanasia? Many Jewish teens probably know what the Pope thinks about abortion, but how many know what Judaism has to say about it? Do Jewish commitments have anything to do with choosing a college? a career? These are the issues our teen-agers face as they grow up. The Synagogue must help them find the answers.

The Synagogue must be the place where our teen-agers can meet friends, grow intellectually and emotionally, have troubling questions heard and find some kind of spiritual direction. What teen-agers want and need as they grow must be found at the Synagogue, for if the Synagogue fails to touch them and provide for their needs, our youngsters will turn away and seek what they need elsewhere. The mandate is clear because the stakes are so very high. Simply and unequivocally, the Synagogue must be an exciting, challenging, relevant place for our teen-agers to be and grow.

• The Synagogue must be a place of learning and growth for *very young children and their parents*.

Little children are "sponges," ready to absorb so much of what is presented to them. So, in their earliest days of physical, emotional and intellectual development, they must be exposed to Jewish life.

The Synagogue needs to provide a variety of learning experiences for specific age groups and levels of development.

A Mommy, Daddy and Me Program is for the youngest children—from birth to two years. With the Synagogue as convener and coordinator, this program brings together infants along with their parents, so that new playmates can be found and new friendships formed. The sessions take on a number of different purposes: play group for the youngsters; training in fine motor and intellectual skills; seminars for the parents with physicians, psychologists and child development experts; introduction to Jewish Holidays and observances.

Parents who feel "cooped up" after the birth of a baby and need "to get out of the house," meet others in the same life-situation. Children form their first relationships around a Synagogue-centered activity. And, at the earliest age, they are exposed to Jewish music, art and stories, and "bombarded" with Jewish sensory experiences, which make lasting impressions.

The PreSchool, for children two to five years of age, is the first "formal" Jewish learning situation. Operating during regular school hours, the Synagogue PreSchool offers basic secular education—including socialization, fine and gross motor skills, reading and counting readiness—*and* introduction to Jewish songs, blessings, holidays, alphabet recognition, Hebrew vocabulary. Along with learning to count from one to ten, to catch a ball, to tie a shoelace and to know ABC's, a Jewish child in a Synagogue PreSchool, learns about Shabbat and Pesach, is comfortable wearing a *kepa,* knows how to say *HaMotzi* and can recite the *Aleph-Bet.* In this way, Jewish learning is gently integrated into whole-life experience and is accepted and expected as a regular part of existence.

A Tot Shabbat Program is for children in the Synagogue PreSchool and for those who, for whatever reason, attend another PreSchool or no PreSchool at all. For an hour each Friday afternoon, children—along with one or both parents—come to learn songs and blessings for Shabbat, light candles, drink grape juice and eat *challah,* hear stories and do craft projects. Children are given a happy, exciting introduction to Shabbat—the core Jewish experience—and parents get to know each other and learn how to make Shabbat a vital part of their homes and families.

Learn Along With Me is a program for parents of children entering the Sunday, Hebrew or Day School at age five, six, seven or eight. Parents who do not have a background in Hebrew, Prayerbook or Jewish history may want to learn, on an adult level, the same kinds of material that their children are learning, in order to share the educational experience. Programs of this kind often fail, because many parents are unwilling to admit their lack of knowledge, so the classes must be attractively and enticingly offered, so as not to offend or embarrass.

Early childhood education forms the foundation for a lifetime of Jewish learning and involvement. There is no better way to have a "Jewish background" than to be exposed to Jewish experiences from infancy. The Synagogue must offer early childhood programs as the natural right of every Jewish child.

At the same time, child-centered programs, offered in an easygoing, non-threatening atmosphere, provide the "road back" to Jewish involvement and learning for young parents who may have "dropped out" of Jewish life after their own Bar or Bat Mitzvahs. Jewish parents still do many things "for the *kinder*," for the children. So, young parents often "come back" to Jewish life when it is time for their own children to enter Hebrew School or PreSchool. As they give Judaism to their children through early childhood programs, young parents may become more and more involved themselves.

Today's Synagogue must assure tomorrow's Jewish future by being certain that the Synagogue is a place where children are welcomed, hugged and loved, and given, as a gift of love, the beauty of their heritage and tradition.

• The Synagogue must be a place that responds to the human needs of its members and to the *unexpected crises* in their lives.

The Synagogue, usually through its Rabbi, has, historically, been successful at reaching out to help its people at time of accident, illness or death. However, the Synagogue must be ready, as well, to respond swiftly and compassionately, to the unexpected crises that strike the lives of its members.

During that economic crises of a few years ago, when

the West Coast Synagogue conducted financial seminars for its elderly members, a Synagogue on the East Coast served its people in an incredibly sensitive way.

Jews of all ages and at all stations of life were losing their jobs. High level managers, company executives and corporate vice-presidents were fired as businesses needed fewer employees, cut back on expenses and weathered the recession. Men and women of talent and competence, with a lifetime of successful work experience, ever-increasing responsibility and financial reward, suddenly found themselves without work. Self-esteem and self-confidence were shattered overnight and productive, ambitious people had no source of income and nowhere to go in the morning.

One Synagogue on the East Coast cleaned up its basement, put in a dozen desks and chairs, a bank of telephones, a few typewriters, a copy machine, a coffee pot and a part-time secretary. Out-of-work executives could come to the Synagogue every day, make phone calls, mail out resumes, have phone messages taken for them and talk with others who were experiencing the same situation and feeling some of the same emotions.

The Synagogue made it much easier for the out-of-work men and women to look for new jobs, by giving them the tools to use in the search. But, most importantly, at a very difficult time in their lives, it gave them a place to go every day, and a sense of purpose and dignity.

The men and women who came to the Synagogue's basement "recruiting office" were grateful, beyond words, for the support they received, and reported that they got new jobs much more quickly than their friends who sat home alone, becoming more and more depressed, day by day.

The Synagogue cannot simply be a place for prayer and study. It must touch the whole human being, in times of crisis as well as in times of calm. It must hear the voices of its people, crying out in times of trouble, and provide a support system to meet very real human needs.

For, only when the Synagogue understands and speaks to its people, in all their complex facets, will it have any relevance or meaning to their lives.

Not every program or activity that the Synagogue offers will be needed by, or will appeal to everyone. So, the Synagogue must offer a *smorgasbord* of programs, each attractive to a particular group or responding to a specific need. The Synagogue will not necessarily be able to create or staff every program that its members request or desire. So, the Synagogue serves as a *facility* and a *facilitator* for the *smorgasbord* of activities, some of which will be instituted and run by the people who use them.

The key issue facing the Synagogue today is not about building buildings or making budgets, but about building and rebuilding human lives. It is a challenge that is worthy of every bit of energy required to find the answers and carve out the solutions. For, how it meets the special needs of special people will determine the Synagogue's place and impact in their lives, now and for years to come.

MORE SPECIAL PEOPLE: WOMEN

The last three decades have seen tremendous changes in the place and status of women in American society. Once relegated to the role of wife and mother, teacher, nurse, waitress, or secretary, women can now do and be whatever they choose.

In Jewish life, thirty years ago, women were the carpool drivers, the Sisterhood ladies, tea pourers and Purim Carnival arrangers. Now, they are Presidents of Federations and Synagogues, professors of Judaica, Executive Directors of communal agencies and Rabbis.

One of the most intriguing questions facing contemporary Jewish life is how the American Jewish community will deal with the increasing *feminization* of Judaism.

The issue of equality for women within Jewish life once raged with controversy and conflict. Now, for the great majority of American Jews, the issue is moot, because women's equality and egalitarianism are accepted facts of Jewish life.

From their beginnings, the Reform, Conservative and Reconstructionist Movements have educated girls in the same way as boys. Throughout the years, women have been given voice and vote in Synagogue politics; serve in every organizational capacity; have full rights on the pulpit and in ritual life, including counting in the *minyan,* coming to the Torah for *aliyot* and leading the Congregation in prayer. Since 1972, more than one hundred women have been ordained as Rabbis from the Reform and Reconstructionist Seminaries and, most recently, the first woman was ordained at the Conservative Seminary. These women serve Congregations throughout the country with warm acceptance and high distinction.

Only in Orthodoxy have women been denied equal access and equal rights. For many Orthodox women, the differing sex roles are comfortable and right. For others, it is only a matter of time until the barriers that stand in their way fall.

Intelligent, knowledgeable, committed Orthodox women know that the laws prohibiting them from full participation in religious life were created through no fault of theirs, but out of the weakness and insecurity of the men who wrote the laws. Women are kept on the other side of the curtain/wall/room during public worship because the *men* are afraid that their concentration at prayer will lapse when they can see and hear beautiful, charming women. Women are excused from "time-bound" *mitzvot,* such as daily prayer and the wearing of *tallit* and *tephillin,* because *men* decided that the women's place is at home, taking care of the babies. It won't be long before Orthodox women, who treasure God and Torah *and* their personal self-respect and dignity, will no longer let themselves be confined to kitchen and bedroom, but will take their rightful place in the pews and on the pulpit.

So, with women's equality within Judaism assured in most places, there are two questions which will challenge the Jewish community.

First. How will the new generation of women Rabbis carve out their unique place in Jewish life?

The first women Rabbis were like the first women anything—doctors, lawyers, corporate executives. They fought for and won the right to become Rabbis, *just like the men*. And, during the first years, the first generation of women Rabbis copied and imitated the work of their male counterparts. Thus, the first women Rabbis were just like male Rabbis, except that they were women. They functioned in all the traditional male roles in all the traditional male ways; they wore male ritual garb; they won respect and acceptance by meeting the standards set for them by men and achieving the results expected of them by men.

But, there *is* a difference between men and women. American society is beginning to understand that women doctors, lawyers, executives need no longer simply imitate men in order to succeed, but can bring their unique characteristics and approaches to their tasks. Women Rabbis are beginning to assert themselves and their femininity in their work, too.

A woman Rabbi need not act like a man in order to be effective. She does not, necessarily, have to wear the same prayer garments—*kepa, tallit, tephillin*—in order to bring sanctity to worship. She does not have to approach her work with male words and male attitudes in order to have equal status. She does not have to give up her inherent and natural instincts in order to be a legitimate and valid servant of God and the Jewish People.

Just think what special understanding a woman Rabbi brings to celebrating the birth of a child, to talking with a teen-ager, to listening to a lonely old man. Think what unique compassion a woman Rabbi brings to comforting a grieving widow, to hugging a troubled adolescent, to empathizing with a frightened bride. Think what unique insights and world-view a woman Rabbi brings to

her preaching. Think what unique instincts a woman
Rabbi brings to establishing her role of leadership and to
affecting consensus and compromise within a group.

The time has finally arrived for women Rabbis to
express their own uniqueness by evincing their femininity. Without fear of rejection and without denying or
stifling their own natures, women Rabbis can now bring
their womanhood and their feminine characteristics to
Jewish life. As they do, the fabric of American Judaism
will be so much richer and brilliantly hued.

The second challenging question is: how will the
people in the Congregations cope with and adapt to the
emerging feminization of Judaism?

The prominence of women Rabbis is not the only
place where the impact of women on Jewish life is being
felt.

Increasingly, the Synagogue is being populated by
women, because women are in the building, at Services
and activities more often than men. Women still drive the
majority of Hebrew School car pools and often socialize or
take classes in the Synagogue while their children are in
School. Women, whose husbands are not interested in
Judaism, (a large and growing group) find themselves
creating the rituals within the home, bringing the children to Shul, volunteering for the committees and organizations within the Congregation and serving on the
Board and as Officers of the Synagogue. Women are most
often the ones to bring their children to Services on a
weekday *Yontif,* while husband/father is at work. So, on
the second day of Sukkot or the seventh day of Pesach, in
many Synagogues, the majority of worshippers are
women and children.

How will women deal with their new role as the
dominant Jewish force, not just in the private domain (the
home), but in the public domain (the Synagogue) as well?
What different attitudes and expectations will women
bring to Synagogue life? What priorities and values will
they bring to worship, education, the political organiza-

tion and structure? What new directions will they set for the Synagogue? How will they define "fellowship" and "community"?

How will the men react to their own diminishing role? Will they want to retain their positions of leadership? Will they come out of the office and back into the Shul to regain their place, or will they continue their benign neglect of Jewish life and institutions? Will they still write the checks while their wives make the decisions?

American women have, in the last decades, "come a long way, baby." The Synagogue has not been immune from the "sexual revolution" which has swept through the society. Old assumptions have fallen and new rules are being formulated. Some of the gains made by women have been hard fought and deservedly won. Others have occurred by default, with women rushing to fill the void left by uninvolved, disinterested men. But, one thing is clear. The feminization of American Judaism, which is taking place at this very moment, should be joyfully proclaimed, because it infuses our faith community with new tenderness, compassion and sensitivity, new energy and new, exciting, unlimited possibilities.

MORE SPECIAL PEOPLE: CONVERTS

One of the Jewish community's greatest failures has been the way we have sought, trained, welcomed and accepted converts. For many complex and convoluted reasons, prospective converts have been discouraged from choosing Judaism; stymied, rather than enthusiastically encouraged to embrace our beliefs and faith community. The path to conversion has been difficult and fraught with obstacles, and, even those who finally fulfill the requirements and formally convert, have often been marked by discrimination and considered "second class."

This attitude may have been understandable in days gone by, when Jews feared and distrusted the gentile world and were reluctant to become too familiar to "out-siders." It may, even, have been understandable when Jews believed that being the "chosen people" meant being superior to those around them because of a special relationship with God. But, in today's open society, when Jews coexist side-by-side with so many other religions and nations, and when Judaism needs all the strength and support it can muster, a negative attitude toward converts is unacceptable and intolerable.

Besides the very human requirements to respect and sincerely welcome those who choose to explore Judaism and become Jews, the stark fact is that converts represent American Judaism's best hope for new growth and new strength. The reality is that the American Jewish com-munity is growing increasingly older and that the birth rate has slipped below the replacement level. Intermar-riage is diminishing our ranks and unless, by some polit-ical miracle, the gates of the Soviet Union open, there is no source of new immigration to augment our numbers. The richest potential source of new Jews—knowledgeable, committed and active—is conversion.

Rabbi Alexander Schindler, the President of the Union of American Hebrew Congregations, the organiza-tion of Reform Synagogues, has been right in his recent call to action. While we need not stand on the street corner "hawking" Judaism to every passerby, we must actively seek out prospective converts, show them the beauty of Jewish belief and practice, eagerly teach and train them, wholeheartedly encourage them to choose Judaism and warmly welcome them to allegiance to the God of Israel and membership in the People of Israel.

There are many reasons for choosing to become Jew-ish. Some convert after their life's philosophical and spiritual search lead them to Judaism. Others convert out of a desire to marry a Jewish man or woman. Still others convert, after having been married to a Jew for a number of years, to bring consistency to family life and child-rearing. Whatever a convert's original motivation, it is a great *mitzvah* for Rabbi and Synagogue to bring a person "under the wings of God" and into the household of Israel.

The course of study and the requirements for conversion differ with each "wing" of American Judaism and amongst individual Rabbis supervising the process. And, there is no doubt that these differences have caused a great deal of confusion and disagreement in recent years.

Most Orthodox Rabbis demand absolute commitment to *kashrut,* Shabbat and Holiday observance and adherence to the laws of family purity. Many Reform Rabbis have been accused of doing "quickie" conversions, with the whole process taking no more than a few weeks. The Conservative Rabbis, who claim conversions done according to *halacha,* Jewish law, are denied access to local *mikvahs,* ritual pools for the ceremony of immersion, by Orthodox Rabbis who proclaim that the conversions are not "kosher."

This "in-fighting" and parochialism has led an age-old question to take on new dimension. It used to be that the answer to "who is a Jew?" was "a person born of a Jewish mother or one who has converted to Judaism." Now, the answer varies. Every Rabbi and *halachic* authority now says, "a Jew is a person born of a Jewish mother or who converts to Judaism through a process of conversion *which I deem acceptable.*" To complicate the matter, the Reform Rabbinate has recently declared that a Jew is anyone born of *either* a Jewish mother *or* a Jewish father, who takes certain public actions affirming his or her Jewishness.

This wide divergence in approach and opinion has led to a serious schism within the Jewish community and could result in complete anarchy. At stake is who will be permitted to marry whom, the legal status of children and, if the Orthodox establishment eventually has its way, who will be permitted to become a citizen of Israel under the Law of Return.

There seems to be but one solution to the disagreements over the conversion process. On local, regional or national levels, Rabbis from every "wing" of American Judaism must band together to create Rabbinic Courts which will supervise all conversions. It is an idea that worked, until recently, with fabulously successful results, in Denver, Colorado. For the common good, Rabbis have to set aside their individual differences, compromise with each other and officiate at conversions which are acceptable to all.

No prospective convert should be caught in the "crossfire" between disagreeing Rabbis or be subject to abuse or degradation from one faction or another. No one who sincerely wants to become part of the Jewish people should go through the difficult, soul-searching and life-altering process of conversion only to be rebuked or rejected by one Rabbi or another. Surely, if Egypt and Israel can settle some of their differences, the American Rabbinate can unite long enough to agree on one acceptable method to bring converts into Judaism.

Once we have settled the technical problem of *how* to bring converts into Judaism, then, the Jewish community must be particularly sensitive to the *feelings* of Jews by Choice.

To convert to Judaism means facing divergent and swirling emotions. It may mean rejection by family, abandonment by friends, loneliness at former holiday times. It may mean desperate desire for acceptance and constant fear of "not doing it right." It may mean being barely tolerated by future in-laws and embarrassment over being the object of whispers and gossip. At the same time, it will mean new-found joy and satisfaction. It will mean fulfilling a life's search and feeling new happiness and inner peace. It will mean new friends, new tastes and smells, new adventures. It will mean a sense of belonging and at-homeness. Always, it will mean a giant leap into the vast unknown.

Converting to Judaism is an awesome, exciting, scary experience. For the prospective convert, it means reaching to the depths of heart and soul. It means real or imagined confrontations with parents, priests and persona. It means dredging up childhood, and breaking away from cherished memories. It means critically evaluating life-long assumptions, throwing away long-held beliefs and slowly carving out new commitments. It means rejecting and accepting; shutting off and opening up; walking out and coming in—often all at once. Converting to Judaism means a highly charged emotional transition which requires gentle assistance, unwavering support and the promise of warm acceptance on the other side.

Therefore, Rabbis, the Synagogue and the entire Jewish community must truly, truly listen to the feelings, the hopes, the fears, the needs and the expectations of prospective converts and respond to them with a warm embrace of approval and welcome.

A young woman, an undergraduate student at a local university who studied for conversion with me, wrote of her feelings in the Jewish Students' newspaper on her campus. She has much to teach us.

> "Jews by birth wonder why anyone would want to be a Jew by Choice. The convert knows the life of a gentile and that oppression (for Jews) is everywhere. But, nowhere else can one find a people based on historical tradition, nationality and religion. Nowhere else can one find such celebration of the Sabbath and nowhere else is humanitarianism valued over redemption of sin.
>
> "In America, there are two emotional facts Jews by birth and Jews by Choice are afraid to face. The first is that converts *do* have particular feelings—special problematic feelings. The act of going to the *mikvah*—dramatic as it may be—rarely makes them feel Jewish. The other difficult fact to acknowledge is that converts feel a special sense of loneliness. During times of Christian holidays like Christmas or Easter, the convert faces choices about loyalty to his/her new

faith or old family traditions. During times of
Jewish holidays, the convert may feel alienated or
used. Once, I was asked to carry something home
from an Oneg Shabbat by a Jewish friend. For
her, it was unthinkable to carry on Shabbas. But,
for a convert, breaking a commandment was
permissible. I felt used and, more importantly, I
felt rejected as a Jew.

"Just as the Jews by Choice have accepted a
covenant encompassing the People of Israel, the
People of Israel must accept a covenant which
embraces the convert. Before a Jew by Choice
can complete the emotional transition to Judaism, feelings of uncertainty and rejection must
be alleviated. No matter if a Jew has been accepted into the covenant for two hours or sixty
years, by an Orthodox Yeshiva or a liberal Reform
Temple, the same sense of caring and acceptance
(from the Jewish community) should prevail.

"Converts are people who respect Judaism
and work hard in all areas of their life to fulfill
their covenant. *Jews by Choice hold the promise
of the future for an assimilated chosen people.*
(italics-mine) They will raise their children in a
loving Jewish environment and educate them in
the observances and spirit of Judaism, because
they have *chosen* to do so. They want to be an
active part of the Jewish community and want to
feel at ease with the life altering transition they
have chosen.

"Equally important is the sense of understanding about Judaism and its traditions which
a Jew by Choice can share with you. Invite one,
just one, Jew by Choice to talk. Ask what he is
studying—and why. You may hear phrases you
haven't spoken since your own Bar/Bat Mitzvah.
You may gain a new understanding of your own
heritage. You may think about Israel as a home-

land, instead of some politically charged piece of land in the Middle East. You just may be rekindled into the loving spirit of Judaism yourself."

The message is very clear. Instead of making it uncomfortable and difficult for non-Jews to choose Judaism, the Synagogue must open its doors and its heart. For, rather than the Jewish community doing converts a great favor by graciously permitting them to join our exclusive "club," they do us a much greater favor—they honor us—by choosing us.

Converts offer us a look at our own Judaism through fresh new eyes. Our Jewish birthright of God, Torah and *mitzvot*—which so many Jews simply take for granted—is so attractive and so precious to converts that, in order to be part of it, they are willing to give up much of what they were.

In a time of crisis of faith, they seek God and find Him. In a time of declining Jewish observance, they eagerly create Jewish homes, participate in Jewish rituals and bring their children to Shul. In a time of dwindling Jewish population, they, and their children, increase our numbers. In a time of diminishing Jewish commitment, they actively seek out and embrace our religion and bring a new spirit and vigor to our People.

For all they do for Judaism, converts ought to be greatly respected and highly honored. The Synagogue must celebrate their conversions and welcome them into the community. Conversion ceremonies, which were once hidden away, private observances, should be joyous public occasions. On the first Shabbas following the conversion, the new Jew should be given an *aliyah*—called to the Torah to recite the blessings—in the presence of the entire Congregation. This Jew, who has freely and happily chosen to accept God and the obligation of His commandments, is at least as worthy to be at the Torah as the thirteen year old who has a Bar Mitzvah because "my parents made me do it." At Services, in the Congregational bulletin and, perhaps, even in the public press, the conversion should be announced and belauded, as a new soul is born into the Jewish People.

New Jews must be encouraged and permitted to bring their own special contributions into Jewish life. Judaism can and does have the right to demand that a convert give up certain beliefs and practices in order to be Jewish. No one can be Jewish and believe that God is divisible into three, instead of uniquely One. No one can be Jewish and go into a church's confessional booth to seek absolution from sin. But, Jews by Choice need not be required to give up all of who and what they are—to become entirely blank slates—in order to convert. Instead, they can offer Judaism the richness and the depth of their own, individual cultural and ethnic backgrounds.

For example: A few years ago, I was teaching an adult class about the observances and rituals of Passover and the highlights of the Haggadah. Because there are so many different customs and traditions surrounding Pesach, I asked people to explain their own family's rituals. I asked, "what do you use on the Seder plate for the *karpas,* the green vegetable?" The answers varied: celery, parsley, lettuce. Then I asked, "what do you use for the *maror,* the bitter herbs?" Again, different answers: horseradish, radish, horseradish root.

One woman, who had converted to Judaism years before from an upbringing as a Spanish Catholic, raised her hand and said, "At our Seder, for the *maror,* we use jalepeno peppers!"

For a moment, there was stunned silence, then dawning understanding, followed by happy grins. Here, a woman who long ago accepted Jewish beliefs and practices, and observes major Jewish Holidays in their traditional way, nevertheless, brings a part of her own background, her own unique ethnicity, into her family's Jewish rituals. Instead of entirely cutting off her past, she retains part of herself by cleverly merging old with new and creating new approaches and modes for Jewish life.

Throughout Jewish history, Judaism has absorbed elements of the surrounding culture into our religious practices. Now, we have the almost unprecedented opportunity to add even greater richness and beauty to the fabric of our faith by encouraging the tens of thousands of converts, with their many and varied histories, to bring in, sanctify and Judaize their own cultural, ethnic and gastronomic backgrounds. If only we let them, Jose Martinez, Mary McCarthy and Dominick Giovanni have as much to give us as we have to give them.

In order to best facilitate the converts' comfortable and complete integration into Jewish life and community, every Synagogue must have a Jews by Choice Support Group. This group is for all converts, prospective converts, converts-in-training, people who are married to converts and people whose children are married to converts.

This group is of immeasurable benefit in helping Jews by Choice make the transition into Jewish life and face sometimes strange, confusing or difficult situations. The group is valuable in many different ways: Someone who converted a year ago can help the person who is studying toward conversion with the details of preparation, dealing with family, the fear of the unknown. Someone who is ready to immerse in the *mikvah* and come before the *Bet Din* can be guided by another who has already been through the experience. Parents whose child is contemplating an intermarriage, or is in love with someone who is considering conversion, can hear from other parents who have faced the same situation. A new Jew who is going to make her first Shabbas dinner or her first Seder table can get advice and assistance from those who have already done it. A woman who has been Jewish for fifteen years, but is now approaching her first son's Bar Mitzvah, can talk with others about how to handle her own Christian parents and relatives in the Synagogue on the day of the *simcha*. Each year, at Christmas and Easter time, when old memories are stirred up and family may exert subtle or not-so-subtle pressure, Jews by Choice can find empathy and strength with others who understand.

A Jew by Choice needs a support group because converting to Judaism—being Jewish—is a continually evolving, life-long process of learning and doing. Every step of the way—one day, one year, one decade—into being Jewish, it is important for the convert to have others of similar experience with whom to talk, share, laugh and cry. And, it is vital that the Synagogue offer ongoing teaching, encouragement, understanding and support, so that the Jew by Choice truly feels fully accepted by the community which he or she has chosen.

At the very beginning, Abraham heard the still small voice of God and the Jewish People was born. Every time a person hears that same voice, in our day, the covenant is reaffirmed and renewed. For their faith, for their personal courage and for their choice, converts deserve the encouragement and respect of the entire Jewish community.

Let Jews by Choice into our midst with warmth and acceptance, for they are our brothers and sisters. They are an important part of our future.

STRUCTURES: INSIDE AND OUTSIDE

In order to succeed at its increasingly complex tasks; provide the fullest, most attractive *smorgasbord* of activities; to best serve the people who seek its services and to attempt to touch the people who have yet to walk through its doors, the Synagogue must revamp its structures, develop new formats and expand its parameters.

• *In certain locales,* Synagogues must *stop duplicating their services and competing* with each other.

It is understandable that pride and chauvinism—and the desire to attract more and more members who provide a larger and larger financial base—compel every Synagogue to do the most and the best it can. But, in cities with large Jewish populations, such as New York, Los Angeles and Chicago, where there are many Synagogues within close geographical proximity, this attitude often produces wasteful duplication and unnecessary competition.

Certainly, each Synagogue must conduct religious Services, for the variations of custom, tradition and melody differentiate one from another and add to the richness of American Jewish life.

But, when a number of Synagogues are located within a few miles or city blocks of each other, they need not all offer a full menu of very similar programs, such as Pre-School, Youth Activities, Senior Citizen Programs and Singles Groups. Instead, Synagogues can combine their efforts and maximize their effectiveness.

While it is necessary for the Synagogue—as an institution—to run a variety of programs to meet many diverse needs, rather than every Synagogue in the same area conducting the same activities, each Synagogue can become a *specialist* in a particular area. One Synagogue can concentrate on programs for older adults; another can specialize in early childhood education; a third can become the expert in youth groups.

This approach has a number of advantages. First, there is strength in numbers. A Synagogue Youth Program that attracts two hundred teen-agers will be able to offer better activities, pay a more highly skilled advisor and have more friends to meet than a Program that has only fifty youngsters. Secondly, there will be great financial savings. Four Synagogues running four separate PreSchools means four sets of expensive equipment, four staffs of well-paid teachers, four very high insurance premiums, four electric bills. One combined program saves Jewish money. Finally, when the collective expenses are significantly reduced, then, with the combined savings, Synagogues can double and triple their program offerings and, thus, their overall effectiveness.

This approach extends to special programming as well. For example, recently, in one city, two Synagogues, located very near each other, each sponsored a major Distinguished Speakers Lecture Series. First, one Congregation established its series. Not to be outdone, not to lose prestige or influence, the second Congregation created a very similar series the very next year. It was a wasteful gesture. Instead of joining together to offer one outstanding series, the two Synagogues played "one-upmanship," competing for attendance and touting their series—and their Congregation—as "the best."

The printing costs and the postage for the announcement brochures, alone, could have sent two or three children to Jewish Day School for a whole year on full scholarship!

Just think how much better it would have been had those two Synagogues combined their efforts. Not only would their own community have benefited, but, with just a little creative vision, their program could have a far-reaching effect.

There is little chance that Jews in tiny or isolated Jewish communities throughout the United States will ever be able to bring a large number of the high quality Jewish "super-star" speakers to their cities and towns. Logistics are difficult and costs may be prohibitive.

So, let the large city Synagogues sponsoring the Lecture Series have the programs professionally video-taped and, then, distributed at low cost to other Jewish communities throughout America. Nothing substitutes for a "live performance," but having a video of a distinguished speaker, talking and interacting with an audience, is better than never hearing or seeing at all.

Here is a perfect place to demonstrate the principle of *K'lal Yisrael,* the totality of the Jewish people, united for the common good, rather than separated by theology, ritual or pride.

There is too much to be done in Jewish life to duplicate efforts, spend money twice or be divided by foolish
competition. When geography and practicality dictate,
Synagogues must join forces and share ventures. For,
when Synagogues unite in purpose, the entire Jewish
community reaps the benefits.

• In *other locales,* the Synagogue should *return to* the
old concept of the *Synagogue-Center.*

Decades ago, the late, great visionary, Rabbi Mordecai
Kaplan, taught the Jewish community how to build
Synagogue-Centers—buildings which have facilities and
programming not only for worship and Jewish education,
but for social, recreational, athletic and artistic activities,
as well. In cities and towns where the Jewish population
is not concentrated into a small geographical area, but is
spread out over many miles, the Synagogue-Center becomes the focal point for Jewish life.

The Synagogue-Center, to be called in its modern
incarnation, The Center for Jewish Life, does not "pigeon-
hole" people's needs into slots called, "religious," "educational" and "cultural," but, instead meets the needs of
the *whole human being.* So, in addition to worship
Services, classes and lectures, The Center for Jewish Life
provides programs for *every age group and every life
situation,* from prenatal to beyond the grave, and *deals
with all the needs* of a human being: spiritual, religious,
educational, cultural, intellectual, emotional, communal,
financial, social, recreational, athletic and artistic.

First, The Center for Jewish Life fulfills all the traditional roles of a Synagogue. Therefore, its buildings have
a Sanctuary, a Social Hall and kitchen, educational centers and classrooms, a library, meeting rooms, a youth
lounge, offices and outdoor play areas.

The Center for Jewish Life also offers recreational and
athletic activities. Therefore, its buildings have a gym, a
swimming pool, a health club, athletic fields and tennis
courts.

The Center for Jewish Life also offers activities in the fine arts. Therefore, its buildings have rooms, centers and studios for art, dance, music, drama, audio and video.

The Center for Jewish Life is sensitive to all life styles and life experiences. Therefore, its buildings have child-care centers; in-town summer camping facilities; a music room and a periodical room; a Museum for the display of permanent and visiting collections of Judaica and art; a Gift Shop to make religious and art objects available for sale; a "kosher store" offering kosher packaged and frozen foods; a kosher snack bar for lunches and simple dinners.

The staff of The Center for Jewish Life is developed to meet the needs of this diverse kind of programming. So, in addition to a Rabbi, Cantor, Educator and Administrator, The Center for Jewish Life has staff specifically trained to work with various age groups: youngsters, adolescents, adults, seniors; social programmers; recreational and athletic coaches; specialists for various programs—music, art, dance, camping and more. The staff should also include a psychologist who works with the various groups, advises the staff and is available, by appointment, for individual and family counseling and therapy.

It might be argued that there is nothing Jewish about a swimming pool or a basketball game and that Jewish money and energy ought not to be wasted on these "frivolous" and "irrelevant" activities. And, certainly, the Synagogue, which has so many important, holy, things to do, need not become involved in these secular pursuits.

It is true. There is nothing Jewish about sports or a dance class. But, when Jews gather to play or relax, it somehow, becomes a "Jewish activity," because Jews are doing it. And, when Jews come together—even for a game—there is always potential for Torah words and God talk. And, at the very least, Jews can find other Jews, make new friends, and (especially for young people:

remember, "dating leads to mating") form new relationships.

It might be further argued that Jewish Community Centers, JCC's, provide all these athletic, recreational and artistic activities, so there is no reason for the Synagogue to duplicate or compete.

It is true. JCC's do all these things. But the JCC is a *secular* Jewish organization. It brings Jews together, (and, increasingly, more and more non-Jews, because JCC's are often beneficiaries of local United Way campaigns, and thus must be open to all people regardless of religion or creed) but it does not offer Judaism—Jewish life style, life rhythms, life values. And, history has taught that Judaism survives not just in the places where there are Jews, but in the places where Jews lead Jewish lives of Torah and *mitzvot*.

At the JCC, the only thing that will happen is that Jews will gather. But, when the very same activities are offered in a Synagogue setting, there is a chance that Jews who otherwise might never set foot in a Synagogue, will be exposed to Torah and Jewish life.

It works like this: People who will not come to a Service or a class, *will* come to a health club, a swimming pool, a card game, a pottery class. When these activities take place at a Synagogue-Center, then, these people will walk past a Jewish library. They will meet the Rabbi in the "schvitz." They will sit next to a "Shul Jew" at the pool, talk, meet a new friend, be invited to a Bar Mitzvah, and, then, come to Shul, where they will see a Service, hear a sermon, meet other "Shul Jews."

Since the majority of Jews are not coming to the Synagogue, the Synagogue must find ways to bring them in. If people will not come to the Synagogue for Services or classes, they may, nevertheless, be enticed by other things they need/want/enjoy. And, once people come into the Synagogue buildings for any reason, they can be exposed to and, hopefully, attracted to participation in religious Services or educational programs, even, if at first, it is only out of friendship or curiosity.

This concept of The Center for Jewish Life has some supplementary benefits.

Currently, the Synagogue is losing many bright, energetic people to interest in other Jewish institutions such as the Federation, JCC's and Old Age Homes. They shy away from participation in the Synagogue because they feel that they do not know enough, or are uncomfortable in a religious setting. The Center for Jewish Life provides an easy, gentle, non-threatening introduction to Jewish life, to involvement in the Synagogue and, eventually to commitment and roles of leadership. The Center for Jewish Life deepens the quality of the Synagogue by helping to produce active loyal members.

Further, The Center for Jewish Life broadens the Synagogue's financial base. Many, if not all, of the social, recreational and athletic activities pay for themselves through users' fees, and often, make a small profit. So, those who use the health club will, in time, wind up subsidizing the Hebrew School. In addition, every person attracted to Synagogue membership who came, originally, for athletic or fine arts programs, increases the Synagogue's financial strength.

The Center for Jewish Life, the Synagogue-Center, is an old concept that has new application, because it makes so much sense. The Center for Jewish Life is for everyone. "Shul Jews" will have their normal experiences deepened and broadened, and those who have stayed away will have good reason to come back.

When it deals with the realities of its people's lives, when it hears *all* needs and responds to them, when it touches minds, hearts, souls and bodies, then, the Synagogue will, once again, be doing its job and Jews will, once again, come through its doors.

• The Synagogue must *extend its services beyond the walls* of its buildings to *meet* a wide variety of *Jewish needs.*

If the price of *kosher food* is too high, making it a financial burden for many people to observe *kashrut,* and keeping many others from choosing to do so, then, to lower costs, the Synagogue can create a Kosher Co-op.

There are many stops along the way in bringing kosher food from farm to table. At each place in the pipeline, there are profits to be made by growers, preparers and conveyors, as well as the long parade of supervisors, approvers and certifiers. At the retail level, many grocers and butchers, especially in outlying communities, claim that, in addition to all the costs necessary to get the products onto their shelves, and their own built-in profit margin, their own prices must be higher yet, because of low volume and slow turnover.

What is worse is that at Holiday time, particularly at Passover, when certified Kosher-for-Pesach food is an absolute necessity for observant Jews, the kosher suppliers have a strangle-hold monopoly and charge highly inflated prices, which the beleagured consumer is forced to pay.

To make kosher food and meat available at the lowest possible prices, the answer is the Synagogue's Kosher Co-op. Buying in bulk, using volunteer labor from the members of the Co-op, eliminating the need for marketplace profits and relying on the local Rabbi's own *hashgacha,* (*kashrut* supervision and authorization) the Kosher Co-op can mean high quality at a fair and decent price.

There can be no price tag to Jewish ritual and observance. When more people can afford kosher food and, particularly, kosher meat, then more people will observe *kashrut.* So, the Synagogue must encourage and lead the way back to *kashrut* by establishing the Kosher Co-op.

• If the costs of *Jewish funerals* are too high, pushing Jews to non-Jewish funeral homes, or to cremation instead of traditional Jewish burial, then the Synagogue can form a *Chevra Kadesha,* a Holy Burial Society, to bring Jews to their final resting place with dignity and honor, without undue financial burden on the survivors. In his book, *A Plain Pine Box,* Rabbi Arnold Goodman, now of Atlanta, describes how he created just such a society at his former Congregation, Adath Jeshrun, in Minneapolis.

Rabbi Goodman and his congregants prove that it is possible for a Synagogue to offer its members a traditional Jewish funeral, complete with transportation, preparation and guarding of the remains, shrouds, a plain pine coffin, a funeral service and burial, for little or no cost. In addition, the Burial Society, called at Adath Jeshrun, the *Chevra Kevod Hamet,* (literally, the Society to Honor the Dead) provides the bond of friendship and support to grief-stricken relatives as they move from the trauma and shock of the moment of death, through making the arrangements and the funeral, into the *shiva,* the seven day period of mourning, toward reconcilation and healing.

The members of the Society, recruited from the membership of the Congregation to this noble task, have returned to a time before professional Funeral Directors and elaborate Funeral Homes. Because the Society is comprised of volunteers, the high cost of funerals—which is greatly attributable to the mortuary's mortgage and upkeep, professional staff and profit margin—is eliminated. The Jewish funeral is, once again, what it used to be—a group of friends attending to the final needs and honors due a deceased member of the community.

By reviving the *Chevra Kadesha,* the Holy Burial Society, the Synagogue can help significantly reduce the high costs of funerals. But, most of all, the *Chevra Kadesha* can, in our time, fulfill its age-old purpose of honoring the dead in the most intimate way and, at the same time, wrap the mourners in the love and warmth of the faith community.

• If *Jewish learning* and *appreciation of Jewish culture* are at a painful low, then the Synagogue must be the conduit through which its members are exposed to current Jewish thought, books, periodicals, magazines, music, film and theater.

Some of the most creative work being done in Jewish life today is in the field of publishing and the arts. Hundreds of books of Jewish interest are published each year. Dozens of Jewish magazines and journals are in print. Scores of films with Jewish themes, plays with Jewish content and records with Jewish music are produced.

Unfortunately, many Jews do not know about these works because only a few Jewish books or movies are so universally popular that they make the best-seller list or are screened from coast to coast. Only two Jewish periodicals have mass circulation—*Hadassah Magazine,* published by Hadassah, and *The Jewish Monthly,* published by B'nai Brith. Each reaches more than one-half million readers. But, the next largest nationally circulated Jewish journal has fewer than 50,000 subscribers.

It is the Synagogue—its Rabbi, Cantor, Educator, teachers, librarian—which knows Jewish books and periodicals, keeps up with new publications, and can introduce its people to the world of Jewish literature, the sounds of Jewish music and the sights of Jewish film and theater.

The Synagogue must have a library which contains classic Jewish texts, histories and biographies, reference works and popular current fiction and non-fiction. It should subscribe to the dozens of Jewish journals which explore contemporary Jewish themes. It can have a constantly expanding collection of records and cassettes of Jewish music, and video tapes of Jewish movies.

Twice or three times a year, a list describing new books, recordings and popular periodicals should be sent to the members of the Congregation, along with information about costs and subscriptions. The Synagogue can negotiate with the publishers for group rates for its members, so that obtaining the books and recordings and subscribing to the periodicals will be as financially attractive as possible.

The professional staff of the Synagogue should cull the best, most important articles from the various magazines, photocopy them (with permission from the copyright holder, of course!) and send them to the members of the Congregation. If a Jew does not come to the Synagogue library and is not interested in subscribing to a journal, then, he can still be exposed to current Jewish thought through the mails, by receiving copies of articles, book reviews and movie critiques.

At the same time, the Synagogue can encourage its members toward creative expression by sponsoring a literary magazine, a music chorale and a drama group. There is great emotional satisfaction in writing, singing and acting, and the Synagogue can be the outlet for its members' talents. There is no reason for a Jew to be forced into a secular or church choir or a community Little Theater group to fulfill his artistic abilities, when the Synagogue can provide the opportunity for Jewish creativity and performance.

There is a great deal of Jewish talent "out there," untapped and going to waste. And, there is a storehouse full of Jewish resources and experiences "out there," unread, unheard and unknown. If people will not come to the Synagogue to find Jewish learning and culture, then the Synagogue must send it to them, so that Jewish lives can be enhanced and enriched through Jewish writing, music and fine arts.

• No Jew's life is spiritually complete until he or she has set foot on the soil of Eretz Yisrael. So, the Synagogue must encourage and make sure that every Jew *travels to the Land of Israel.*

For almost 2,000 years, Jews prayed daily, "In Your mercy, O God, return us to Your holy city of Jerusalem."

And, as Yom Kippur ends and the Pesach Seder concludes, we shout, "Next year in Jerusalem!" Now, after all those years of waiting and praying, Israel is ours. And, you must go! Not every Jew can or wants to make Israel a physical homeland, but, Israel is, for each and every Jew, our spiritual homeland. And, it is to that spiritual center that you must make pilgrimage.

You need to walk through the dust of your history. You need to see the sun splashing golden rays against the holy stones. You need to hear the sing-song of young boys learning a Talmud text and the wordless melody of old men at prayer.

You need to see the blue and white flag proclaiming freedom and the soldiers who, for the first time in 2,000 Jewish years, mean not destruction, but protection. You need to see some of the 167 million trees that the Jewish National Fund has planted in Israel's soil since 1948, and the irrigation systems that have made fields of flowers and food out of the desert sands.

You need to stand at the border and feel the guns pointing at you from the other side and you need to meet 18 year old boys who are ready to defend with their lives. You need to feel pride in a conquerer who gives rights and respect to the vanquished, and assures religious freedom and equal access to the holy sites of every faith. You need to visit the classrooms where Jewish and Arab children sit side-by-side with full equality and dignity, and walk in the Arab villages which have electricity, running water and toilets for the first time.

You need to make new friends by talking to the brave mother and her children on the border *kibbutz;* the father whose son was killed liberating Jerusalem; the doctor at Hadassah Hospital, seeking the cure for cancer; the bus driver who takes you from place to place, but spends sixty days a year maneuvering a tank through the Golan; the young scholar at the Hebrew University who programs a state-of-the-art computer with medieval Rabbinic Responsa; the newly married couple who ignore overwhelming inflation and put a down payment on an apartment; the 14 year old whose life ambition is to be a paratrooper.

You need to have a personal, intimate connection to Israel, so that when you hear of fighting or a pipe bomb exploding, you hold your breath until you know your friends are safe; so that when independence is celebrated each year, you sing and dance with joy; so that when Israel needs the help of the American government, you can tell your Senator that he must vote to protect your brother and sister, your closest friends.

The Synagogue must sponsor regular trips to Israel, not just as sightseeing vacations, but as spiritual pilgrimages. The journey should be led by the Rabbi, or other staff professional, who shares the task of conducting the tour with an experienced, passionate, inspiring Israeli Guide.

Each trip should be preceded by in-depth study sessions, complete with readings, maps and slides, so that every participant will be a prepared, knowledgeable tourist. The community should help celebrate the departure of each pilgrimage group with prayers and blessings on the Shabbat immediately before takeoff. Each trip should be followed by a series of gatherings to share feelings, pictures, experiences and commitments.

Families should be encouraged to travel together. Parents give their children an extraordinary gift of legacy and destiny by bringing them to Israel. Whenever possible, three generations of a family should travel together, for there is something very special about grandparents and grandchildren praying together at the Western Wall and walking the Land of Israel with each other.

The Synagogue can help make the cost of traveling to Israel easier to afford by establishing an *Israel Fund* for each child who enters Day School or Hebrew School. Each year, parents pay an extra $100 in addition to tuition. That money is put into a special interest-bearing trust account. Over the years, the annual contribution and the accruing interest will grow into a sizeable sum which will, eventually, make up a large portion of the cost of bringing a child to Israel.

It is a spiritual journey of a lifetime, so one of the great and sacred tasks of the Synagogue is to help each and every Jew say, as did the Psalmist of old, "I was joyous when they said to me, 'Come, let us go up to the House of the Lord' "—to the Land of Israel, to the holy city of Jerusalem.

• The Synagogue must help its people *meet new friends* and *form new relationships*.

Synagogues come in many different "flavors." There are Orthodox, Conservative, Reconstructionist and Reform Congregations. There are Synagogues with thousands of family members and Synagogues with only a handful of families. There are Synagogues in decaying, inner-city neighborhoods, in crowded urban areas and in sprawling suburbs. There are Synagogues in neighborhoods where hundreds, thousands, of Jews live within a few blocks of each other and Synagogues that serve Jews spread out over the countryside, linked only by miles of superhighways.

Jews come in many different "flavors" too. But, most Jews, like most all human beings, have some very similar longings: for health and prosperity; for satisfaction from work and gratification from play; for intellectual stimulation and emotional fulfillment; for loving and being loved; for needing and being needed; for sharing and caring and touching; for friendship, for happiness and for inner peace.

The Synagogue must be the place for finding and making friends, for enriching life through human relationships.

In Synagogues with members who live far from each other, in a number of different communities, the Synagogue must provide an opportunity for people to meet on an informal basis.

Over the years, my Synagogue has sponsored a program called "Dinner for Eight." Very simply, the Synagogue sends out an invitation to its members to get together with three other couples, or seven other people, for dinner. With the invitation is a questionnaire which asks for name, neighborhood, job or profession, children's ages, previous places of residence and special interests. The questionnaire asks by which, if any, of those factors the people would like to be "matched" with others.

The Synagogue office makes the "matches," asks one of the group to host the dinner at home and to invite the others. The dinner is either served by the hosts, or can be "pot-luck." Since we are concerned, as a Congregation, with the laws of *kashrut,* we ask that the dinner be *pareve* and/or dairy.

There is never a "shill" from the Synagogue asking for anything—not attendance at Services, participation in programs or contributions of money. The dinners are simply a chance for people to meet.

As each group of eight gets together and shares a dinner, people get to know each other and new friendships are begun. From these dinners have come both casual and lasting relationships, which include reciprocal dinner invitations, family outings, baby-sitting co-ops, a tot's play group, sharing of Holiday celebrations and business contacts.

Each year, Dinner for Eight is one of the Synagogue's most popular and successful programs because it touches a real need—for people to be with people.

Synagogues with many hundreds, even a thousand or more, members face a different kind of challenge. A Synagogue of this size can often seem large, foreboding and impersonal. New members have a hard time "breaking into" old friendship groups and cliques. So, instead of being warm, welcoming and inviting, the Synagogue seems cold and aloof.

To solve this problem, some fifteen years ago, Rabbi Harold Schulweis of Encino, California, created, in his

Congregation, the Synagogue-based Chavurah. The Chavurah responds to so very many needs, in such a brilliant manner, that it is an idea which has spread to Synagogues throughout the country and is now an integral part of American Jewish life.

The Synagogue helps to establish small, independent groups within the large Congregation. Each group, consisting of approximately ten couples, is called a Chavurah (plural: Chavurot), which means "friendship group." The Chavurot are formed, originally, by matching people with similar interests and needs.

Some Chavurot are formed so that people can study Judaism together; some so that families can get together to celebrate Holidays; some for appreciation of Jewish music or theater; some out of special interests, such as a group of Jews by Choice, or a group concerned about social action activities.

Most Chavurot meet at least once a month and each Chavurah democratically administers its own affairs, sets its own schedule and agenda and decides on its own activities and issues for discussion.

As with all families or groups, some people participate actively; others less so. Some people grow very close; others maintain more casual relationships. As they become friends, the members of the Chavurah share in each other's lives: at times of joy such as the birth of a child, Bar Mitzvahs and weddings, and comfort each other in times of trouble and sorrow. The Chavurah becomes the extended family—with all the great benefits and the occasional traumas that families bring.

As the years go by, the Chavurah evolves and grows. Some members leave; others are invited in. The interests and the needs of the members change and, so, the focus of Chavurah activity changes as new priorities develop.

The Chavurah has been accused of fragmenting a Synagogue into small, independent groups that may work at cross-purposes and have no loyalty to the unity of the Synagogue-community. This problem is easily solved by a Chavurah Council, an active arm of the Synagogue, which coordinates the work and the direction of all the

Chavurot and assures participation in the programs and activities of the Congregation.

By reducing the thousand family Congregation into subgroups of ten families, the Chavurah has been tremendously successful in *humanizing the Synagogue* by replacing the cold, impersonal atmosphere of many modern Synagogues with warmth, caring and sharing. The Chavurah is the way that the Synagogue can really help Jews feel connected to each other and fulfilled in friendship.

In some Synagogues, small groups form to reach out to other human beings by fulfilling traditional *mitzvot* of Judaism: welcoming the newcomer, hosting the traveler, visiting the sick, caring for the aged and comforting the mourner.

A Synagogue sponsored Mitzvah Chevra, a friendship group dedicated to doing a specific *mitzvah,* is of great benefit to both the *mitzvah* receiver and the *mitzvah* doer.

In our increasingly mobile society, people often move from place to place, leaving family, friends, familiar surroundings and warm memories behind. A Synagogue Mitzvah Chevra which welcomes newcomers to town can mean the difference between confusing loneliness and easy integration into a new community. A member of the Mitzvah Chevra can help with things such as finding shopping centers, grocery stores and the library, and introductions to school principals, doctors and Hebrew School teachers.

A traveling business-person may find him or herself away from home, in a strange city, on Shabbat or a Jewish Holiday. A member of a Mitzvah Chevra which hosts travelers can offer an invitation to dinner and accompany the guest to Shul. During the summer, when families vacation throughout the United States, this Mitzvah Chevra can welcome visitors to the community and help them find the best hotels and restaurants, the best sights to see, and offer assistance in case of emergency.

A Mitzvah Chevra devoted to visiting the ill and infirm brings company and good wishes to a hospital bed, a nursing home room or a home sickbed. A patient's spirits can be lifted and recovery hastened by a visitor bringing good talk, a book, a newspaper, some flowers and a warm smile.

The elderly, in an Old Age Home, want visitors for conversation and companionship. And, the elderly confined to their own homes may need help with shopping and errands, keeping up with correspondence and bills, a ride to a doctor's office or, simply, a daily telephone call to have someone say "hello." A Mitzvah Chevra devoted to serving the elderly can do all these things and more.

At the time of death, the *Mitzvah Chevra,* a part of the Chevra Kadesha, helps the survivors with the myriad of details planning the funeral, contacting relatives, picking up friends at the airport, providing out-of-towners with a place to stay and the many other arrangements that must be made. Most of all, Mitzvah Chevra members offer the mourner caring friendship and a warm hug.

In our day, so many of these sacred tasks have become the responsibility of the Rabbi—who represents the community in the performance of *mitzvot.* But, to return to the real meaning of *mitzvot*—people reaching out to people—individual Jews must return to accepting the responsibility and the privilege of caring for each other.

Again, Rabbi Harold Schulweis has created a model for training Jews to do these practical *mitzvot.* His Para-Rabbinic Program has a cadre of people who spend a year or more preparing to do *mitzvot* by learning Jewish law, modern psychology, counseling and communication skills, and acquiring the tools to make them effective helpers.

But, whether a person is professionally trained or is simply motivated by the stirrings of his or her heart, the goal is the same: for Jews to find each other in friendship and cradle each other in caring.

It was one of the greatest advertising commercials of all time. It applies not just to the telephone company, but to the Synagogue, which, as one of its primary concerns, must provide the vehicle for its people to "reach out and touch someone."

- The Synagogue must *reach out to those who cannot or will not come through its doors.*

There are many Jews who would like to be in a Synagogue, participating in worship Services, but cannot, for they are ill and confined to a hospital or nursing home. The misery of their illness is compounded by the misery of loneliness and isolation from family, friends and the Jewish community. Visitors help, but they are just not enough.

To help address this problem, about five years ago, I created The Video Synagogue. Through the modern technology of video tape. The Video Synagogue brings the Synagogue, the community, the Rabbi and Cantor, and the familiar Service and melodies right into a patient's own room through his television set.

The Video Synagogue is a forty-five minute Friday Evening Shabbat Service. There are traditional prayers, responsive readings—with easy-to-read graphics appearing on the screen—melodies, songs and sing-a-longs, and a short inspirational message. A full Congregation, of people of all ages, participates with the Cantor and me, giving the viewer the sense of being in a Synagogue with a community of Jews. The Service is in full color, set in an artistically attractive Synagogue. Beautiful and picturesque background scenes add to its visual and aesthetic appeal.

Hospitals and nursing homes rent or buy the video tape and show it to their patients—through the facility's closed-circuit system—on each room's television set. No Jew need feel lonely any longer. Now, on Shabbat and major Holidays, the Jew who cannot come to the Synagogue can have the Synagogue come to him. He—and his family visiting with him—can participate in dignified, joyful, uplifting worship Services along with a community of Jews.

Does The Video Synagogue work? Here are some reactions from those who have seen it:

From hospital patients in California and Maine:

"I enjoyed the Service very much. This is a program whose time has come and I'm glad to see it."

"Excellent Service. Very much enjoyed. You are to be congratulated for providing this much appreciated and very needed Service."

From a Jewish Hospital Chaplain in Chicago:

"Patients and visitors have been very receptive to the program! People said they were singing along and enjoyed the Service. It really added a lot to the Hospital and brought the Shabbat spirit here."

From a Protestant Hospital Chaplain in Arizona:

"The response to the program is good, very good. Thank you for your keen insight into the needs of our patients. You are meeting a deep need."

From a Rabbi and Educator in Washington D.C.:

"It is a splendid example of using the latest technological, scientific advances to the service of God and Torah."

But, even The Video Synagogue is not enough. There are others, besides hospital and nursing home patients, who would like to be in a Synagogue, but cannot: those confined to their own homes by illness, infirmity, weather conditions, lack of transportation or old age.

There are others who, for a variety of reasons, are not in a Synagogue. These are Jews who are away from home, traveling or on business; are in prison or otherwise incarcerated; live in small isolated towns, far from a Synagogue; are on military bases, without a Chaplain; are single or recently divorced or widowed and feel uneasy and, perhaps, unwelcome in a large, communal group; lack Jewish education and skills and feel out of place and uncomfortable in a Synagogue setting.

These are Jews who must and can be reached—at home, in a jail cell or in a hotel room—and touched by Judaism's ancient teachings and contemporary vibrance.

And, there are those who have chosen to stay away from the Synagogue: the 70% of American Jews who do not belong to a Synagogue and the more than 50% of all Jewish school-age children who receive no formal Jewish education. Because they have been "turned off" and will not attend formal Jewish insitutions in traditional settings, these Jews are denying themselves part of their heritage and authentic identity. And, the Jewish community is being deprived of their participation and creative contributions to Jewish life.

For American Judaism to be revitalized and for the Jewish future to be assured, these Jews must be sought out wherever they are—physically, intellectually and emotionally—and touched by warm, exciting, challenging, stimulating, uplifting and meaningful Jewish experiences and, once again, be "turned on" to Jewish life, celebrations and values.

• The answer to reaching all these Jews is *television*.

The Christian community has used television for more than twenty years to preach its word. The Jewish community is far, far behind. While Judaism's message is very different, the use of the medium of television to touch hundreds, millions, of Jewish lives and souls, can be much the same.

There have already been significant attempts and worthy successes in using television to teach Jews about Judaism in a positive, pleasant, exciting way.

Most notably, for many years, the Board of Rabbis with the Federation in Chicago has produced Emmy Award winning Jewish television. In recent days, a number of separate but similar endeavors in Jewish television have been undertaken, utilizing the emerging availability of Cable TV: a nationally syndicated program from Israel called, "Hello Jerusalem;" cable networks in Los Angeles, New York and Boston; locally produced programming, often through community access, most notably "Aliyah" in the Boston suburb of Needham; and attempts and proposals for national programming by organizations called National Jewish Television and Dr. Moshe Waldok's Corporation for Jewish Broadcasting.

I, myself, created a California non-profit religious corporation called The Television Synagogue with the idea of bringing worship Services and segments of Jewish education and fine arts—much like The Video Synagogue in hospitals—to all Jews, wherever they may be.

In their infancy, all these fledgling attempts at using television to the widest extent to teach Judaism's message have a number of things in common: they are created by individuals working independently with similar ideas, but with little coordination with each other; they are working independently, without any major Jewish organizational or entrepreneurial support; they are greatly ambitious, but under-financed; they are still searching for the right vehicle and instrumentality to make them most effective.

The logical solution is a Jewish Broadcast Network which can reach every cable-subscribed household and every backyard satellite dish in North America through satellite up-link.

A Jewish Broadcast Network, which can be on the air

for eight, ten, twelve hours a day, can bring all types of Jewish programming right into millions of homes: worship Services, like The Television Synagogue; educational programs of all kinds for children and adults; cultural programs of Jewish music, art, dance, drama; old and new movies; live Jewish news programs; interview shows; political forums and much, much more.

We need to coordinate all the efforts; tap the best and most creative people in the television, entertainment, electronic and satellite industries; find the most experienced business people; and seek out corporate sponsorship to make a nationwide Jewish Broadcast Network a reality.

This is Jewish Outreach at its greatest potential. Hundreds of thousands, millions, of Jews can be reached and touched with the beauty of Jewish religion, education, culture and Peoplehood—simply by turning on a television set.

The benefits can be tremendous, for individual Jews, for the Synagogue, for the entire Jewish community and for good will and new understanding that will come from the non-Jewish community.

Not everything the Synagogue can and must do can take place within its walls, no matter how wide and diverse those walls be. So, quality Jewish television can help expand the walls of the Synagogue, by reaching out to Jews in new ways—via new technologies—and by enveloping them in the beauty of Judaism and the warmth of the Jewish community.

It is no longer enough for the Synagogue to be a monolithic institution, providing one kind of programming, available only to those who walk through its doors. The needs of the Jews of America have become widely diverse and are constantly changing and evolving. So, with new awareness coupled with even newer creativity, the Synagogue must reach out to all Jews—wherever they may be—by widening its horizons, extending its boundaries and enlarging its vision.

SPIRITUALITY AND VALUES

Over the past four or five years, I have spoken to hundreds of people who have joined my Synagogue. To each one, I asked the same question: "Why are you joining this Congregation?"

Some of the answers were flattering: "We are joining because you are the Rabbi."

Some were practical: "We are joining because the location is convenient."

Some were philosophical: "I used to belong to a Reform Temple, but I am really more comfortable in a Conservative Shul."

Some were expected: "We are joining because we want a good Jewish education for the children."

But, one answer was different. It was an answer that, frankly, in all my years in the Rabbinate, I have seldom heard. And, yet, I heard this answer, often tentatively and haltingly given, over and over again, until I realized that there is a new trend emerging.

The answer is this: "I am joining this Synagogue because I feel a need to do so. I haven't been religious; I haven't been active in a Shul before. In fact, I have hardly been inside a Synagogue in years. But, I'm feeling a new awakening within me—to seek out my beginnings, to touch my roots, to find some answers to life's hard questions. I'm feeling a need for something beyond myself, for something spiritual. I am wondering if I can find God."

Even in this age of great intellectualism—when we still worship at the altars of Harvard and Stanford and pay homage to the gods of education and rationality—many Jews are coming to realize that where knowledge ends, belief begins, and when there are no more words, music fills the soul.

There is a great hunger for the sacred. There is a yearning for moral right. There is a craving for the transcendent, for the enduring, the eternal. There is a searching for truth, for meaning, for God.

It is a tenor that is returning to America. Recently, *Time* magazine reported that the religious sensitivity of the nation can be measured by the kind of facilities that Churches and Synagogues build. In the 1960's, the emphasis was on education, so construction concentrated on schoolrooms and playgrounds. In the 1970's, the emphasis was on fellowship, so social halls and multipurpose rooms were built. In the 1980's, the emphasis is returning to worship, so, before anything else, Churches and Synagogues are building their *Sanctuaries*.

So many Jews have tired of the secularism, the permissiveness, the thrill of the moment. You want more. You want something beyond yourself, something higher and deeper than yourself.

So, you came to the Synagogue, seeking the holy, the timeless, the infinite. You came seeking direction, certitude and faith.

And, the Synagogue failed you.

Instead of God-talk, you got book reviews and political editorials. Instead of God's call to compassion and justice, you got the prevailing social agenda. Instead of God's ethical mandate, you got pop-psychology, which, no matter what you do, insists, "I'm OK. You're OK."

You got a dues bill to pay, a building-fund pledge card to sign, and raffle tickets to sell.

And, you said, "Isn't there anything more than this?"

And, when the Synagogue answered you with resounding silence, you went elsewhere, because your soul cries out for meaning; your whole being waits for answers.

So, Jews stopped wrapping in *tallis* and *tephillin* to *daven* and turned, instead, to the cults, to TM and est and yoga, because there, you found heightened spirituality, answers to your questions and a reason for being.

A mantra is nothing more than secular *nusach*, prayer melody, but, these "secular religions" give you something that Judaism has not. They "fill the hole in your soul." They awaken within you a sense of purpose. They give you structure and direction.

Never mind that a weekend at est costs almost as much as a year's Synagogue dues, (clever entrepreneur, that Jack Rosenberg!) you listen to the gurus with rapt attention, bordering on awe, because they "show you the way" to wholeness and spiritual contentment.

Judaism has all the forms, all the rituals and observances to assure emotional fulfillment, all the answers to satisfy spiritual hunger. But, somehow, somewhere, Judaism and the Synagogue lost the ability to convey to you the great beauty, meaning and satisfaction which your religious heritage has to offer.

So, now is the time for the Synagogue to reclaim its rightful and unique role.

The Synagogue must speak the words of the ages; words that, in your spiritual quest, you desperately want to hear. Put most succinctly by the late, great, revered teacher of our time, Abraham Joshua Heschel, the message is as simple as it is profound: "God is of *no* importance, unless He is of *supreme* importance."

Everything the Synagogue does—every Service, every class, every program and activity, every technique and technology used to bring people through its doors and to reach them where they are—is for but one reason: to teach, in word and deed, that we are God's children and that He has a plan for us. He wants us to live and make known His *mitzvot*, His code of behavior, His moral imperative. He wants us to hear the voice echoing from Sinai and share its dictum in our time and place: God wants us to "perfect the world under His kingdom," to be His partners in making our world a place of holiness and harmony, of peace and love.

How can the Synagogue fulfill this mandate? How can it bring religious values back to a secular world? How can it speak to people who hear only the voice of their guru? How can it sing God's song over the drone of a mantra?

First, the Synagogue must go, with interest and respect, to see where its people are. The Synagogue must explore the cults, yoga, est, TM, the health club and all the other "secular religions," and see what the attraction is, what these groups and practices offer, what they have that Judaism does not.

Then, instead of trying to replace them, let the Synagogue learn from them, by taking the best of the modern disciplines and stirring them together with Judaism to find new forms, new modes, new expressions of faith and spirituality. Instead of rejecting the "secular religions"— and, by extension, the people who flock to them—let the Synagogue use what they have to teach us in order to enlighten and strengthen Judaism.

Most importantly, the voice of moral right must, once again, be heard from the Synagogue.

No Rabbi who stands on a pulpit is ever "six feet above contradiction," but, no Rabbi who takes his commitment seriously can be without conviction.

So, the Rabbi must speak not out of whim or fancy, but from the teachings of Torah. He must convey God's enduring ethical mandate and teach, from God's moral perspective, what is right and what is wrong.

For, when people, once again, come to accept God as the ultimate moral authority, then, all the other issues of human existence fall into place, one by one, because the value system by which they will be decided is His.

Of course, the danger inherent in this position is that anyone and everyone can say that he knows God's will and speaks for Him. Such moral certitude can lead to arbitrary narrowness and, in the wrong hands, to persecution and genocide. But, to whom shall we Jews listen? The Pope? Jerry Falwell? The Ayatolah? Or, shall we listen to God's Torah interpreted by the Sages, hallowed by the ages, taught by our Rabbis?

For us, the answer is clear. The commands of Torah are as brilliant and as compelling today as they were, when they were first spoken, more than 3,500 years ago.

Other moral codes have had their moment of glory in human history. But, now, they gather dust on library shelves, or are quaint displays in museum showcases.

Only Torah values have transcended time and place, because they reflect God's inherent understanding of human nature—our fears and foibles, our needs and hopes, our problems, passions and possibilities. His truths are truths for all time. His universal ethic applies to all people.

Torah teaches us human dignity; how to care for our spouses, our parents, our children, for our friends and our enemies, for each other and for ourselves.

Torah teaches human rights: how to treat the widow, the orphan, the deaf and the blind, how to share what we have with the poor and the oppressed, what justice and righteousness really mean.

Torah teaches us how to be human and humane: to raise our existence above the level of the animals, to discipline our passions for food, for sex, for accumulating possessions, to control our desire to either dominate or to take the easy way out, to demand, from ourselves, the best that is within ourselves.

The Synagogue must, once again, be infused with spirit and with action. Torah values must be reflected in word and in deed.

The Synagogue must hear God's command to feed the hungry and clothe the naked by having a continuing collection of food and clothing for those who need it.

The Synagogue must hear God's command to free the oppressed by working on behalf of Soviet Jewry and the Jews in the Arab lands, by putting pressure on governments to release those who are held in political bondage, wherever they may be. Fifteen years ago, almost every Synagogue had a gigantic banner, proclaiming to every passerby, "Free Soviet Jewry!" What happened to those banners? Where are they now?

The Synagogue must hear God's command for peace by working to avert nuclear holocaust, so that the rainbow continues to shine.

The Synagogue must hear God's command for honesty and integrity in business by making sure that all its own affairs and dealings are conducted above reproach, that money can never buy undue influence, that lack of money can never bring disfavor or disgrace.

If not from the Synagogue, from where will God's ethical mandate be lived and taught? If not to the Synagogue, to where shall Jews go to hear God's word and be wrapped in His love?

The Synagogue has lost its way, but, if only it will listen, its people can lead it back. For, contemporary Judaism is being infused with a spiritual renaissance, brought about by people whose hunger for the sacred demands immediate nourishment.

So, the Synagogue must learn that to be popular, it need not fall prey to the latest fads. Rather, it must fulfill its unique role—to articulate God's ethical and spiritual mandate to His people.

Then, people will, once again, turn to the Synagogue as the repository and the teacher of enduring values and eternal truths, and their sounds of spiritual renewal and newfound contentment will be heard throughout the land.

ADMINISTRATION

To accomplish the many varied and complex tasks of providing for the religious, educational, cultural, social and human needs of its members, the Synagogue must be run in an efficient, businesslike manner.

The Talmud understood, centuries ago, when it taught: "If there is no flour (meaning: food, sustenance, money), there is no Torah."

A Synagogue can conduct the best religious Services, offer stimulating classes, have a Rabbi who is an outstanding preacher and a compassionate pastor, but, if it cannot pay its light bill in February or its teachers' salaries in May, it cannot exist.

Admit it or not, like it or not, the modern Synagogue is a business. Even small Congregations have budgets reaching toward $250,000, and large Congregations, complete with Building Funds, have multi-million dollar financial statements.

The time of being solely dependent on good-hearted, well-meaning volunteers in order to function is over. The time of existing from contribution to contribution, hands constantly out, hoping that "the Lord will provide" is at an end. The Synagogue must be administered with competence, skill and fiscal responsibility. The Synagogue must be managed and funded like any other well-run corporation.

Most every American Synagogue is organized on the principle of "participatory democracy." Anyone who pays dues becomes a "member" of the non profit religious corporation and has co-equal voice and vote.

The problem is, that in running a business, participatory democracy is a flawed and imperfect system.

What other business gives its consumers a vote on how its affairs are conducted?

If you own a restaurant or a supermarket or a bookstore or a clothing boutique, you make all the decisions which affect your business. You pick the location, sign the lease, purchase the inventory, hire and fire the staff, do the advertising and keep the financial records. If your business succeeds, you reap the profits. If your business fails, you are liable for the consequences.

Even a large corporation, which has "gone public," only allots its shareholders a vote proportional to the number of shares they own. A stockholder with 100 shares of the company does not have the same say, enjoy the same benefits or assume the same risks as the company's founder and chief operating officer who owns a million shares.

Yet, the Synagogue permits its customers to make all its decisions. People with little or no Jewish background decide on ritual practice. People with little financial investment and no financial accountability or responsibility make fiscal policy.

So, instead of being able to concentrate on doing its best to offer a product that will satisfy its customers and keep them coming back for more, the Synagogue has become the arena for petty fights and power plays, where responsible decision-making has been replaced by ill-conceived majority rule and high school-like popularity contests.

Since the Synagogue is a business, and must be run like a business, *let it be a business!*

Here's how it can work:

A Rabbi and a group of like-minded individuals come together to establish a Synagogue. But, instead of being organized as a participatory democracy, it is formulated as a proprietary business.

The ten or twenty individuals start up, "own," run and maintain the Synagogue.

Their business—their Synagogue—offers a product: in this case, religious Services, Jewish education, programs and activities for Jewish culture, recreation and socialization.

Their customers are the people who "join" the Synagogue in order to take advantage of the products which it offers.

As in any other business, the creators of the business form the management group—which they may call a Board of Directors, a Council of Trustees, or anything else they choose. The management group makes all the decisions regarding the conduct of the affairs of the Synagogue. The members of the Board are, therefore, solely responsible for creating the programs, hiring the staff, setting the fees, advertising, promoting and fiscally managing the Synagogue. They, and they alone, decide on matters of policy for the corporation.

At the same time, the members of the Board must be personally responsible for the fiscal stability of the corporation. As with any other business, the "owners" must provide the "seed money" for start-up costs. Then, the Board members must know that dues, fees and donations will cover only 75%–90% of the Synagogue's annual

operating budget. Therefore, they must commit themselves to work on fund-raising projects to make the Congregation financially secure. In addition, each Board
member must be willing to cover or make up, in a proportional share, whatever cash deficit remains at the end of
any fiscal year. This can be accomplished by: making a
contribution to the Synagogue, or by lending cash to the
Synagogue, or by guaranteeing a bank loan, on a line of
credit, through personal signature and personal liability.

Thus, people who make the key fiscal, policy and
personnel decisions for the Synagogue are, at the very
same time, personally accountable and responsible for
their choices and actions.

As with any other business, the creators of the business, the members of the Board, are the permanent
managers of the Synagogue. The Board elects its own
officers from amongst its members. Each Officer (usually
a President, Vice-President, Secretary and Treasurer)
serves in place for as long as he or she chooses. When the
Officer decides to relinquish the Office, he or she remains
on the Board, while another member is elected to fill that
Officer position.

If a member decides to leave the Board after fulfilling
all his legal, financial and moral obligations to his fellow Board members, then, the Board, itself, replaces (or
chooses to leave vacant the place of) that member. Just
as if a partner leaves any other business, here, too, the
remaining partners choose his replacement.

Members of a Board of this type *will* choose to leave
the Board (but, certainly not the Congregation) from time
to time, when they are satisfied that they have made a
positive, worthwhile contribution to the organization. A
few members will leave the Board when they realize that
their positions on issues or their argumentative style
isolate them from the others. Rather than continuing to
disagree or confront, they will leave the group.

The people who "join" the Synagogue are, in legal
terms, not "members," but "licensees." They pay a

set fee (dues) in exchange for use of the facilities and the services which the Synagogue provides. If they use a specific program or offering of the Congregation, which has an additional fee attached to it, (such as the Hebrew School) then, they pay the additional users' fee which has been set by the Board.

People who join the Synagogue, therefore, do not automatically receive a vote in the affairs of the Congregation. They simply take advantage of the programs and activities offered to them.

But, rather than having less influence than in a traditional Synagogue structure, the members, here, actually have tremendous power. In a democratically run Synagogue, each member gets only one vote amongst many hundreds of others, and usually accedes to the will of the majority. But, in a proprietary Synagogue, which is solely dependent on the continuing satisfaction of its members, any member who is unhappy can "vote with his feet" by leaving the Congregation.

So, the Synagogue must please its consumers, or they will stop coming, stop paying dues and stop making contributions. And, if enough members are dissatisfied, then the Synagogue will not have enough "customers," the "cash register" will not ring up sales and the Synagogue will be "forced out of business."

Thus, in order to "keep the customers coming," to keep the members happy and content, the Board must continually listen, solicit opinion and be acutely sensitive and responsive to the needs and the desires of the members.

The old adage "the customer is always right" may not be completely accurate, but, in the proprietary Synagogue, it is a principle by which to live.

The Board engages a Rabbi to serve the traditional Rabbinic roles *and* to be the Executive Vice-President, Chief Operating Officer, of the corporation.

To facilitate the Rabbi's work, a number of provisions are made:

First, the Rabbi is one of the permanent, voting members of the management group. This clearly defines the relationship between Rabbi and Congregation. The Rabbi is not simply an employee of the Synagogue, but a partner in its business.

Secondly, the Rabbi's authority as *mara d'atra,* religious authority, is clearly stated. Once the basic religious posture of the Synagogue is decided, the Congregation does not need a religious committee, or to take votes on what is kosher, what ritual practices are permitted or prohibited, or how Services are conducted. Those decisions belong to the Rabbi.

Next, as Executive Vice-President of the corporation, the Rabbi is responsible for the day-to-day administration of the Synagogue, with all the duties and responsibilities of an Operating Officer.

The Rabbi submits a yearly budget to the Board and monitors its progress by spending allocated dollars and making adjustments in spending if actual income does not meet projections.

He hires and fires all employees of the Congregation. Functioning as Rabbi, he is the expert in religious and educational matters. Who better, then, to know the professional qualifications and competence of an Educational Director, a classroom teacher or a Torah Reader? Functioning as Executive Vice-President, he must work, on a day-to-day basis, with the secretary, the janitor, the bookkeeper. Who better, then, to hire his own support staff?

In practical terms, when the Congregation hires a major employee, (Cantor; Educational Director) particularly if that person were to be moving from out of town specifically for the position, the Rabbi would have the members of the Board meet with, question and be happy with the individual before making the final decision. The Board's approval is important to confirm the Rabbi's selection and to make the new professional employee comfortable with the people he or she will serve.

All employees are directly responsible to the Rabbi, who, in turn, is directly responsible to the Board for their function. If, for example, the Congregation grows large enough to need an Executive Director to assist the Rabbi in conducting the daily business of the Congregation, then, that Executive Director would be supervised by and responsible to the Rabbi, not a Board or committee. Just as in any other business, the top professional hires the help he needs, oversees their work, and, then, is, ultimately, responsible to the Board for their performance.

Finally, in recognition of the Rabbi's unique and integral role in this kind of system, to protect his position and to give him peace of mind and security, the Rabbi is given a life tenured contract.

A life-tenured contract is a tricky document. In reality, it really only protects the Rabbi, for if the Rabbi chooses to leave the Congregation, there is little the Congregation can do to make him stay.

However, because a secure position for the Rabbi is key to the success of this kind of organizational structure, a life tenured contract must be created.

Here are some suggestions for the agreement:

The contract outlines the Rabbi's duties: traditional Rabbinic functions; *mara d'atra;* Executive Vice-President and Chief Operating Officer; specific operating responsibilities. Thus, these provisions are not left to verbal understanding or even By-law articles, but become part of a contractual agreement.

The contract provides for compensation and benefits: salary; pension; life and disability insurance; medical insurance; auto allowance; convention and travel; professional dues; vacation and sabbatical.

However, these "usual" provisions need not be just a legal formulation, but deserve a certain level of humane sensitivity.

For example: if a Rabbi dies during the course of the contract, let his widow and dependents receive medical coverage for a period of three or five years following his death. It costs the Congregation only a few thousand dollars, but it speaks volumes about respect and concern.

Another example: the Congregation's intent is to

assure the Rabbi's financial security and dignity at the time of his retirement. The Rabbi's pension, to which the Congregation contributes over the years, should, hopefully, provide that dignity and security. However, a long-term contract is written many years before retirement, and it is impossible to know what the economic conditions will be at the time of the Rabbi's retirement. So, let the contract acknowledge that it may be necessary and desirable for the Congregation to supplement the Rabbi's pension with additional stipends during his retirement. Again, a very human and humane touch.

A very difficult issue to determine in crafting a life contract is how to determine compensation for an agreement which may span twenty or thirty years.

The solution is to set salary figures for a three or four year period, and, then, in the last year of that arrangement, set new salary numbers for the next three or four years.

What happens, however, if the Rabbi and the Board simply cannot agree on salary numbers for the next three or four year period? What if the Rabbi wants "X" and the Board offers "Y" and the two just cannot find common ground?

In many cases, this situation would result in hard feelings and, perhaps, termination of the contract. But, here, the desire is to continue the relationship. So, there must be a quick way to overcome the impasse, while treating each party as fairly as possible.

The solution? Baseball Arbitration!

In Major League Baseball, when a team and a player cannot agree on a salary figure, the issue can go to a specific kind of arbitration. The situation can be the same with Rabbi and Congregation.

If the Rabbi and Congregation cannot agree on new salary figures, then, each appoints an arbitrator. The two arbitrators choose a third. The Rabbi and the Congregation each submit to the arbitrators their proposed salary numbers with all supporting data. The arbitrators must choose *either one* of the two sets of figures. The arbitra-

tors *cannot choose a third number or a compromise
number*.

That's how it works in baseball and that's how it can
work here. When both parties know that the arbitrators
must choose one or the other of the numbers and cannot
choose a compromise middle figure, it keeps both parties
honest and straight in picking fair numbers. The impasse
can be swiftly broken, and the Rabbi and the Congregation can go back to their work, having dealt with each
other with respect and integrity.

There is one more contractual area which must be
faced. Even with a life-tenured contract, there may be
reasons that the Congregation wishes to terminate its
relationship with the Rabbi: moral or financial impropri-
ety; habitual neglect or willful breach of his duties.

However, if a Rabbi's employment were to be termi-
nated under a provision such as this, there is good reason
to assume that the Rabbi might not agree with the Congregation's definition or interpretation of his conduct.

So, to adjudicate that potential dispute, without
having to resort to the civil courts, the contract should,
again, set up an arbitration panel. The panel decides if
the termination is justified or wrongful. If the panel
decrees the termination to be wrongful, then, once again,
Baseball Arbitration is used in order to establish compensation to which the Rabbi is entitled for wrongful termination.

There is one exception to all the provisions of protection granted to the Rabbi by a life-tenured contract. Since
the Rabbi functions as Executive Vice President of the
corporation, he must be able to be evaluated by his
employers/Directors according to a scale of judgment
normally set for corporate managers. Some of the performance measurements, in a Synagogue setting, might
include: membership recruitment, membership reten-
tion, accuracy of financial forecast, budget monitoring
and relationship with employees. Thus, if the Rabbi is to
function as a businessman, his success can be measured
by the success of his business practices.

To maintain the spirit of the contract, which protects

the Rabbi from being subjected to capricious judgment, clear, objective standards of performance must be set out at the beginning of each fiscal year so that the Rabbi and the Directors articulate and agree upon their expectations in advance. When he meets his goals, the Rabbi fulfills his duties. If he fails to meet them, he becomes subject to the same consequences as any other corporate manager.

A life-tenured contract acknowledges the unique interconnection between Rabbi and Congregation, makes fair and reasonable provision for just compensation, benefits and mutual protections, and raises the level of the relationship between Rabbi and Congregation to new heights of respect and dignity.

The proprietary Synagogue works because it makes sense.

The Synagogue is run by its "owners"—the Board members who are committed to the successful operation of the Congregation. Over the years, these Board members learn the information necessary to manage a nonprofit religious corporation. They get to know each other's personality traits and positions on issues. They come to meetings not to create confrontations, but to solve problems. They have a personal investment of time and money in their venture, and they are directly responsible and accountable for their actions.

The operations of the Synagogue are not left to chance or volunteers, but are put in the hands of an expert—a Rabbi who is a trained authority in Jewish religious and educational matters and (if not yet, then, must be) a specialist in administering a non profit religious corporation. The Rabbi, whose career and personal life are intimately bound up with his decisions and success, is given the authority and the autonomy to function, and becomes the master of his own destiny.

The greatest winners in the proprietary Synagogue are the people who become members, to take advantage of the Services, Schools, programs and activities. Instead of having to become involved in the politics and pettiness which characterize so many Congregations, they are treated to the finest Jewish enterprise which a group of deeply committed fellow Jews can create for them. In a Shul without politics, there is more time for Torah!

Lest you think that the proprietary Synagogue is but an ivory-towered idea, a utopian theory that has no possible basis in reality, let me tell you that it exists.

For the past five years, my Synagogue, located in suburban San Diego, has functioned just this way.

So far, the purpose and the expectations have been more than fulfilled.

From the outset, the Congregation was able to define and articulate its goals of providing warm, participatory religious Services; innovative, creative Jewish education for all ages; and a *smorgasbord* of programs and activities to meet a variety of needs.

The organizational structure has been widely accepted in the community. The founders of the Congregation have put the Synagogue on a firm financial base and accept continuing management and fiscal responsibility. Members who join the Congregation are pleased to be exempt from political responsibility and decision-making, while, at the same time, they understand their true "grass roots" power to influence the course which the Synagogue takes.

The "proof" of success—as with any other business—is in the "numbers." So, consider: in five short years, in an area of San Diego County where one Congregation had struggled for years just to maintain itself, and another, literally, closed its doors for lack of support, this new Synagogue has more than 250 member families; a Hebrew School of 125 children; three Youth Groups; a dozen or more ongoing programs, groups and activities; and a community of participating, happy Jews.

To be sure, there have been problems, nagging questions and difficult issues. Some original assumptions have been thrown away. Some plans have not worked out. Some ideas have failed.

But, because of the structure, problems can be addressed quickly; new plans can be formulated swiftly. The concept develops and redevelops, sometimes overnight. The fine-tuning goes on constantly; the Synagogue continually evolves.

What have been, and continue to be, some of the problems?

First, the permanent Board is not really permanent. Certain stipulations limit the capacity of someone to join the Board, but there is no impediment to leaving the Board.

The continuing success of the proprietary Synagogue depends on the proprietors—the members of the Board—maintaining their original purposes and commitments. When one or more of the founders choose to leave the Board, after a period of hard work and dedicated service, replacements for them must be found who agree to the same "ground rules," who share the same vision and are willing to assume the same obligations.

New leadership is hard to find. Because of the financial requirements, potential Board membership is restricted to a certain group of financially able people in the Congregation. Many of the people within this group are so busy and successful in their own businesses or professions, and in a variety of community causes, that they are not able to spend time in Synagogue work. Others, whose commitment to Jewish life and interest in Synagogue affairs would make them fine candidates for Board membership, cannot make the personal financial commitment necessary.

So, the group of prospective new Board members is limited and the Synagogue often finds it difficult to identify, interest and bring into leadership roles the "second and third generation" of Board members, and engender their enthusiastic and enduring commitment.

This leads to, perhaps, the most difficult issue. People become active in a Synagogue when they feel a sense of involvement. Given the proprietary structure, people can get involved in Services, Schools, programs and activities. But, if they do not feel involved in the political structure—if everything is done for them by members of the Board—then, they feel little responsibility to working to solve any problems—programmatic or financial—which the Congregation might have. The attitude is, "they (meaning the Board) are providing this Synagogue for me. I come and 'buy' their product. I have no responsibility to the function of the organization, other than to pay for what I use."

Now, the reality is that this is the attitude of most people in *most* Congregations, whether they have a vote or not. However, there is a small percentage—5%?, 10%?,—for whom the lack of responsibility may mean the lack of involvement and commitment. It is to touch these people that the Synagogue must continue to grapple with the question: how to best maintain the organizational structure of the Congregation—which works and satisfies most everyone—and, at the same time, create an atmosphere that offers involvement which leads to commitment?

One possible solution was to create the President's Advisory Council. In order to listen to the needs and the desires of the membership in an organized way, twenty-five people, representing a wide cross section of the Congregation, were appointed to meet with the members of the Board four times a year. They were asked for advice, counsel, criticism and suggestions. In this way, the membership, through the members of the President's Advisory Council, had voice, if not vote.

As the Congregation grew larger, the sense was that, once or twice a year, there should be a public forum for all the members to gather. These forums give the growing membership a place to be heard and result in many good suggestions and ideas being offered. The expectation is that, when things are fine, few people will come to these forums, but, if there are significant problems, a number of people can be expected to show up and, presumably, their input will be most helpful.

Another solution to the question of involvement in the

proprietary structure is the creation of another tier of the Synagogue Board. A Congregational Cabinet can offer real participation and responsibility to many people, who cannot make the financial commitment to Board membership, but whose involvement in the affairs of the Congregation will be invaluable.

The Congregational Cabinet can consist of the Presidents of the Synagogue's auxiliary organizations: Sisterhood, Men's Club and Hebrew School Parents' Associations. In addition, other members can be appointed with specific portfolios, corresponding to committee chairmanships in other Synagogues: Membership and Hospitality; Adult Education; Public Relations; House; Youth; Special Events. Finally, a number of "at large" members can join the Cabinet.

The Cabinet can deal with specific issues of programming and activities for the Congregation, revolving around the portfolios held by the members. The Cabinet can also discuss and offer recommendations about issues brought to it by the Board of Directors.

To give real voice to the members of the Congregational Cabinet and the members of the Congregation, the members of the Synagogue can be granted, by the Board of Directors, the power to elect three or four members to the Board. These members can serve on the Board with full voice and full vote. They will not have the same financial responsibility as the other members of the Board, but, their accountability to Board membership can be measured in requirements to recruit new members, to work on fund-raising programs and to actively serve on working committees of the Board.

Ways must be found to offer members of the Congregation more involvement, as a means of insuring more investment and commitment in the Synagogue.

Next, the necessity of raising funds to make up the difference between income from dues, fees and contributions and necessary expenditures is an increasingly difficult burden.

The realization has come that fund-raising activities

will depend more and more upon sophisticated, professional approaches, rather than well-meaning, (and, personally obligated) but inexperienced volunteers. Current thinking is that a fund-raising program of the nature and scope necessary to keep the Congregation financially healthy, will take the services of a professional fund-raiser to plan and execute.

The Synagogue needs to take a lesson from universities, orchestras and symphonies, hospitals and other public institutions which engender contributions and fund-raising through the work of an experienced, talented professional, who is a member of the staff.

Finally, sooner or later, the Congregation will have to face the question of larger facilities. The Synagogue is rapidly outgrowing the rented quarters in which it operates and must consider the need to buy or build.

Most of the members of the Board do not want to mount a "traditional" Building Fund Campaign. Many have been involved in Synagogue Building Funds before, and few want to do it again. Further, this is a "young" Congregation, with many members in their 30's and early 40's—paying large mortgages, private school fees and contemplating college tuitions—with little discretionary income for large contributions. Finally, there is the question of whether or not the members of a proprietary Synagogue—who have no real responsibility to the institution—would respond to a public appeal for a Building Fund.

Therefore, as the Congregation faces the need to expand, it seeks alternative ways of financing a purchase or construction. One possibility is the formation of some kind of limited partnership which would be created to buy or build the Synagogue facility, and then, lease it back to the Congregation. In this way, the partners can take advantage of whatever tax benefits may be available, and the Congregation will get its facility, as long as it can handle the yearly debt-service. The partners might even get a small return on their investment, if they put some

Synagogue-related revenue producing commercial space (bookstore, deli, gift store) on the property.

The corollary of that plan is some kind of joint venture on a piece of land large enough to accommodate the Synagogue facility and other residential or commercial construction, which would generate enough income to help finance the Synagogue. For example: homes for sale or rent could be built surrounding the Synagogue; a small strip shopping center could be on the property; a high rise building could contain the Synagogue and rental space for shops and offices.

Since no plans are made, no solutions can be offered, as yet. However, just as the Synagogue was structured in a new, exciting, creative way, a new, exciting, creative way will be found to finance a building program and provide the Synagogue with the facilities it needs.

The proprietary Synagogue solves a whole array of problems which has plagued the contemporary Synagogue, and it creates a new set of challenges that even its founders could not have anticipated. Yet, as each new problem is faced and overcome, the structure evolves and grows to new heights of sense and success.

The laws of your State governing non profit religious corporations may prohibit creating the proprietary Synagogue exactly as described here, because some statutes demand that every member of a Church or Synagogue have a vote in its affairs.

But, if this business-like approach to running a Synagogue makes sense to you, then the best legal minds in your community can find the ways to work within your local laws. Or, if the State laws are truly restrictive, then work to have them changed. After all, government laws regarding religious matters are on the books to help and protect us, not hinder us.

Perhaps only some portions of the proprietary Synagogue appeal to you. Perhaps there is another prototype which you can devise that will work better for you and your Congregation.

But, one thing is clear.

With some brilliant and notable exceptions—in Synagogues where there is dynamic and committed Rabbinic leadership, coupled with well-informed and dedicated lay leadership—in most places, the "traditional" Synagogue structure is too political and too flawed by inefficiency to take the American Jewish community into the decades ahead.

Significant change must be made swiftly and forcefully. We cannot be afraid of old proscriptions. We cannot be intimidated by old inviolate injunctions.

We must learn from the best and most successful business practices how to design, organize and administer an efficient, effective Synagogue. There must be a new model for a new age.

There is too much Torah waiting to be taught, learned and lived for Shul politics to get in the way any longer.

RABBIS

To preside over the newly developing, multi-faceted Synagogue, a new generation of Rabbis must emerge. The piety of the *Rebbe* and the learning of the *Rav* will no longer be enough. A Rabbi must now be thoroughly trained and expert at a wide variety of disciplines and skills in order to be the professional capable of leading the Jewish community into the future.

No matter what new abilities are required, the Rabbi must continue to be the master of Jewish learning and law. His education must steep him in Bible, Talmud, *halacha* and Jewish history. He must have the integrity of depth of Jewish knowledge and the authenticity of Rabbinic scholarship.

Happily, to help insure competence, the Reform and Conservative Seminaries now require their students to spend a year studying in Israel, immersed in Hebrew language and nurturing a life-long connection to the Land and the People of Israel.

But, the modern Rabbi needs many other proficiencies in order to serve the needs of a modern Congregation.

Therefore, the curriculum of the Rabbinical Seminaries must be immediately revised and restructured. In addition to the traditional course of study, every Rabbi must have:

- the equivalent of a Master's Degree in education, complete with specific training in educational theory, pedagogy, curriculum development and educational administration;

- the equivalent of a Master's Degree in psychology and social work, complete with skills in group work and communication, and training in individual, child, marital and geriatric counseling;

- the equivalent of a Master's Degree in business and finance, complete with training in preparing and monitoring operating and capital budgets, administration, marketing, advertising and public relations.

With these disciplines added to his education, the Rabbi will, at least, have the academic background to prepare him for the real-life challenges which will face him in the pulpit.

To further prepare the Rabbi for the realities of his profession, the Rabbinical Seminaries must invigorate their teaching staffs.

Most Rabbinical students plan a career in the pulpit. But, the faculties of the Seminaries are made up of Rabbis who, for the most part, have spent their lives in the world of academic scholarship. They, themselves, have not served in a pulpit for decades, if ever.

Book learning is not enough. A Rabbinical student must be taught the practical skills of Rabbi-ing. And, his teachers must instruct from their own, up-to-date experience, not just from theory or distant memory.

Therefore, every Rabbi-Professor, in every Seminary, must be required to spend at least four months every five years as a Rabbi-in-Residence at a major Synagogue. There, under the supervision of his colleague, the Congregation's Rabbi, the Professor should preach from the pulpit; officiate at *brises*, baby namings, weddings and funerals; train Bar and Bat Mitzvah students; counsel troubled members; meet with Boards and committees and plan and execute programs.

Then, when the Rabbi-Professor returns to the Seminary classroom to teach future Rabbis what it means to be a Rabbi, he will know what he is talking about!

Even with all the changes in curriculum and with better versed instructors, no amount of classroom learning will ever be able to prepare Rabbinical students for the realities of the Rabbinate.

No medical student learns to do surgery only in a classroom; no law student learns to try a case only from a textbook. And, no Rabbinical student can learn what it means to function as a Rabbi, even in five years or more of Seminary courses.

The small Congregations, which Rabbinical students serve on weekends, simply do not provide enough exposure or variety of experience to be sufficient training ground.

Therefore, for one full year following ordination, every new Rabbi must be required to serve as an intern in a Master Synagogue, under the tutelage of a Mentor Rabbi.

Let each "wing" of American Judaism designate its thirty or forty most talented, experienced, successful Rabbis, and let that Rabbi and his Synagogue be the place where newly ordained Rabbis train.

Under the watchful guidance of the Mentor Rabbi, the newly ordained Rabbi will preach and teach; officiate at life-cycle ceremonies; function with different age groups;

develop programs; counsel; work with Boards and committees; and learn Synagogue administration.

This internship has many benefits: The Master Synagogue gets an enthusiastic new Rabbi each year, who brings fresh ideas and unique perspectives to the community. The Mentor Rabbi shares his wealth of experience with a new generation and hones his own skills as he teaches. Like a medical intern, the new Rabbi's skills and confidence will grow rapidly and significantly, while, at the same time, his mistakes will not be too costly. And, the American Jewish community will get what it deserves—Rabbis trained academically and experientially to be the very best they can be.

The Seminaries' responsibility to the men and women they train, and to the Jewish community they prepare them to serve, cannot end on the day of ordination. The Seminaries must make sure that the Rabbi is capable and qualified throughout his career.

So, like doctors, lawyers, accountants and many other professionals, a Rabbi must be required to take continuing education courses, in order to keep his ordination diploma valid.

The Seminaries must set up minimum standards for course work in Hebrew, sacred texts, areas of Rabbinic specialization and practical skills. Classes and seminars can be taken in a variety of settings—local colleges and universities; week-long institutes; summer programs; supervised independent study—with course reports being sent to the Rabbinical School. A Rabbi will be required to take a proscribed number of courses within every five year period in order to have his Rabbinic "license" accredited and renewed.

Without the Seminary's re-accreditation, a Congregation should not be permitted to keep a Rabbi, any more than it could hire him initially without proof of Rabbinic ordination.

In this way, the Rabbi can be assured that his learning

is constantly renewed in a systematic, organized fashion and that he will be continually aware of new developments in his field. The Congregations can know that their Rabbis' knowledge and skills are refreshed and up-to-date.

Thus, the dictum that "the study of Torah supersedes everything" can have real application and meaning.

The relationship between Rabbi and Congregation is so vitally important, so intimate, so, hopefully and expectedly, forever, that it is very much like a marriage. So, how do Rabbi and Congregation find each other and make their *shidduch,* their match?

Each "wing" of American Judaism has a Placement Service, made up of representatives of its Rabbinical and Synagogue organizations, which recommends Rabbis and Congregations to each other.

Most of these Placement Services have "ground rules" by which they operate.

For example: a Rabbi within three years of ordination can be recommended only to a Congregation of 300 or fewer families. As he gains more years of service and experience, he becomes eligible for larger and larger Congregations. Not until he has been a Rabbi for ten years, may he apply to the largest Congregations of 1,000 or more families.

This rule makes certain sense. It gives a Rabbi a chance to grow and mature in his profession and it offers the opportunity for career advancement based on seniority. However, this rule inhibits the free market by prohibiting the "super-star" "rookie Rabbi" from getting the kind of position which he can handle and deserves.

A further inhibition to the free market is that each Placement Service recommends only eight or ten candidates at a time to a Congregation. Only if the Congregation rejects all ten candidates will the Placement Service recommend another group.

Why should a committee sitting in New York decide on who may or may not apply for a position? By what criteria is the eighth candidate recommended, while the ninth is not? How can the Congregation hire any one of the initial applicants, knowing that a more suitable person might be in the second group?

Let the free market system work. Let anyone who is interested in a particular job apply and be judged, accepted or rejected on his own merits.

And, let the process of Rabbinical selection use the most up-to-date technologies. Currently, a Congregation learns about a Rabbi from a resume—words written on a piece of paper—and through whatever personal, word-of-mouth recommendations it can garner. Because of rising costs and budget limitations, often, only a few of the applicants for a particular position are actually given face-to-face interviews.

Let every Rabbi applying to every position provide not only a written resume, but an interview video tape. The video tape should feature the Rabbi answering a certain set of predetermined questions; preaching a short sermon and, then, using ten or fifteen minutes to "sell" himself by describing and displaying his own unique talents. In this way, an interview committee can see and hear a Rabbi and get a sense of his abilities and personality.

At the same time, the Congregation should prepare a video tape introducing the Synagogue and the community. This video tape should feature a history of the Congregation and a tour of its facilities; short interviews with the top leadership and members of the professional staff; a statement about the practices, programs and goals of the Congregation; and a "Chamber of Commerce" tour of the community in which the Synagogue is located. In this way, the Rabbi can learn about the Congregation, community and people he may serve.

Then, tele-conferencing should be used to further interview the candidates. Without having to spend large sums of money for airplane and hotel bills, a Congregation can meet a dozen or more Rabbis, question and interact with them, and both Rabbi and Congregation can see if the "chemistry" between them is there.

Only after video tape and tele-conference interviews, will one or more candidates be invited to the community for further talks and the new Rabbi chosen.

These methods of meeting job candidates are currently in use throughout the business and academic worlds. There is no reason why the Synagogue should not take full advantage of the same kind of techniques to assure that Rabbi and Congregation meet in the best possible way.

In defining the working relationship between Rabbi and Congregation, the life-tenured contract for the Rabbi, described earlier, is of great *mutual* benefit because it not only gives *him* security and peace of mind, but, also imposes a certain discipline on the *Congregation*.

Throughout Jewish Europe, for hundreds of years preceding World War II, and in Israel and in England today, a Rabbi is appointed for life. The Congregation and the community know that the Rabbi's authority is established, and that he can teach and preach without fear of jeopardizing his livelihood.

Only in America are Rabbis hired and fired at whim, subject to constant evaluation and judgment. Only in America do the very people whose lives he is supposed to influence and change, hold the power to uproot the Rabbi and send him packing.

Only in America does there seem to be a new "golden rule" in regard to Rabbis. "He who has the gold, rules." The power is not with the Rabbi's call to moral right, but with the Congregation/employer who controls the checkbook.

This attitude is symptomatic of the breakdown of authority, the disdain for leadership, the insistence on "doing your own thing" that has swept through America. But, it must end. America is slowly learning that it needs guidance, direction and structure. And, the Jewish community is coming to know that it needs strong, forceful, unafraid Rabbis to lead.

The Jewish community must swiftly come to under-

stand the wisdom of Rabbi Israel Salanter, the founder of
the Musar Movement in the mid 1800's, who taught: "A
Rabbi whose community does not disagree with him is
not really a Rabbi. And, a Rabbi who fears his community
is not really a man."

Or, put in modern terms by Rabbi Lawrence Kushner
of Sudbury, Massachusetts: "In any power struggle a
Rabbi has with his or her Congregation—even if he wins,
he loses. And, in any struggle over issues of spiritual
integrity or moral probity—even if he loses, he wins."

The life-tenured contract gives the Rabbi the autonomy and authority he needs. The life-tenured contract
teaches the members of the Synagogue the truth about
themselves: that they cannot go "Rabbi shopping" every
time their Rabbi issues a ruling they do not like; that they
cannot condemn or dismiss him when he speaks a message they might not want to hear. The life-tenured contract assures the Rabbi that his next paycheck will come
and that his children will eat. So, unafraid to speak the
truth, the Rabbi can throw away the book reviews and
pop-psychology and return to preaching God's ethical
mandate to His people.

The life-tenured contract which greatly benefits both
Rabbi and Congregation should be speedily and happily
written in Synagogues throughout the country.

Yet, this is not to say that, on the day of ordination,
every young Rabbi should automatically, be handed a
position with life-long security, for not every Rabbi has
the competence, the learning, the skills, the personality
and the charisma—or the desire—to lead a Synagogue, or
to deserve a long-term arrangement.

There will always be a place in the Rabbinate for the
scholars, the teachers, the authors. Their expertise will
produce our generation's contribution to Jewish scholarship and learning. And, there will always be a need for
Rabbis who are chaplains in the military, in prisons, in
hospitals and health care facilities. Their compassion will
bring God's love in moments of crisis and despair. The

scholar and the pastor will do their work, in the places that are the most productive and comfortable, and they will be compensated and protected by a grateful Jewish community which needs their services.

But, in the Congregations, the free and open market system will prevail. The Rabbis who are capable of serving and administering the modern Synagogue, in all its complexities, will rise above their peers and earn the rewards and securities that their successes command.

Other Rabbis will settle into positions which are compatible and commensurate with their abilities.

The way the Christian Church assigns its priests and ministers can teach the Jewish community how to best utilize the talents of individual Rabbis. Christian clergy specialize in specific areas of ministry. Churches have a Senior Pastor and, then, a number of assistants: a youth minister; a music minister; a counseling minister and more. Rabbis, too, can develop their own talents and specialize in limited areas of the Rabbinate.

While some Rabbis will lead Synagogues—with all the responsibilities and rewards that executive leadership entails—others will serve specialized needs, and be compensated and protected according to their role.

Not too long ago, Rabbis were paid a pittance. Salaries were abysmally low; health and medical coverage, haphazard, and pensions, almost non-existent. The Jewish community thought that it was treating its Rabbi well when the tailor gave him a suit for *Yontif;* the butcher, a chicken for Shabbas and the merchant, a doll for his daughter's Chanukah gift.

Happily, in the past decades, the Rabbi has come to be regarded as a professional, with needs and rights to decent compensation and benefits.

Employment benefits—such as comprehensive health plan, life and disability insurance, and pension—should form the *foundation* of any financial agreement between Rabbi and Congregation. These benefits are not simply "perks" to sweeten a "package-deal," but must assure the Congregation's concern for the Rabbi's dignity and peace of mind in illness and old age.

The Jewish community, today, is filled with too many horror stories of how Rabbis have been treated, to leave their welfare to chance or good will promises.

Item: The widow of a distinguished and prominent Rabbi, who had served his Congregation for more than three decades, was told, soon after he died, to move out of the Synagogue-owned house. The Rabbi and his wife had lived in that home for thirty years; their children had grown up there; every room was filled with her memories. And, worse, she had little money and nowhere else to go. But, instead of graciously permitting their Rabbi's widow to live in her home and buying a new house for the new Rabbi, the Congregation insisted that she move out, so that her husband's successor could move in.

Item: A Rabbi, who had served his Synagogue for more than twenty-five years, reports that he and his wife eat meat only once a week. On the social security he receives and the tiny pension provided by his Congregation—which had paid virtually nothing into a pension program on his behalf all those years—the Rabbi simply cannot afford to buy meat more often. He went to the Board of his Synagogue and said, "Since my pension is so small, would you consider giving me an extra $200 a month, as retirement income, so that I can have enough to live decently?" The reply? "Oh, no, Rabbi. We can't do that. We need all the money we have to pay your successor's salary. You know, we have to pay him more, as a starting salary, than we ever had to pay you."

Need more be said?

And, Rabbis must be paid well—very well—for the jobs they do.

Most Rabbis would not mind working 50, 60 or 70 hours a week, at their difficult, emotionally draining jobs, if they felt that they were being justly compensated. But, they look around at doctors, lawyers, accountants—other similarly educated and hard working professionals—and they see incomes double and triple their own. And, when they live from paycheck to paycheck, they wonder if it is all worth it.

The Rabbi has no opportunity to build equity; no profit sharing; no stock options. He has only today's salary. And, yet, the Rabbi has all the expenses that his contemporaries have and, at the same time, must survive in a social setting created by the community he serves. So, the Rabbi must be compensated well enough to live commensurate with the standard of living of his Congregation and community.

However, the burden for paying the Rabbi ought not to fall on his Congregation alone. The Rabbi serves his own Synagogue, but, he is expected to be active in Jewish causes and organizations throughout the community. Everyone calls upon the Rabbi for his participation: the Federation and its agencies such as the Bureau of Jewish Education, the Old Age Home, the Jewish Family Service; Israel Bonds; Jewish National Fund; hospitals and university campuses; Churches and ecumenical organizations; unaffiliated Jews; Hadassah, B'nai Brith, ORT and more.

So, the community, which utilizes the services of the Rabbi should, through its Federation, share in paying him. Every Synagogue should be given a yearly stipend, from the Federation, toward its Rabbi's salary. In that way, those who benefit from the Rabbi's work will join in compensating him for it.

No one who entered the Rabbinate expected to become wealthy. But, unlike some Christian clergy, no Rabbi ever took a vow of poverty, either. There is no reason why any Rabbi should not be able to afford Jewish Day School tuition, or have to drive around in an old car, or deny his children the best camps and colleges.

For his devotion to them, for his hard work and for his successes, the Synagogue and community must pay its Rabbi very well. Then, in the ways of the marketplace, his own professional worth will be confirmed and his financial security and dignity will be assured.

A Rabbi can conduct just so many Services, teach just so many classes, prepare just so many Bar Mitzvah boys before the weariness of repetition, tedium and boredom set in. The very qualities that the Congregation most admires in its Rabbi—independent thought, innovation, commitment to ideas—can be stifled and lost in the dreariness of the everyday.

So, the Rabbi must be encouraged by his Congregation toward his own intellectual growth and creativity. There must be understanding and respect for the time and energy that the Rabbi needs to learn, think and create.

One Rabbi who, for a generation, led a large, prestigious Congregation, and, at the same time, produced incredibly valuable, popular scholarship tells this story:

When he was working on a particular book, the Rabbi decided to come into his office each day at 8:00 a.m. instead of his usual 9:00 a.m. He used the two hours, from 8:00–10:00 to do his research and writing.

He instructed his secretary to tell anyone who telephoned between the hours of 9:00 and 10:00 that, "the Rabbi is studying. He will get back to you as soon as he can." Often, the caller would say, "I need to talk to him for only a minute or two. If he's just studying, it won't matter if you interrupt him. Please tell him that I'm on the phone."

After being interrupted, time and time again, the Rabbi devised a new strategy. He told his secretary to tell any caller, "the Rabbi is in conference." That was different. The reply became, "Oh, if he's in conference, please don't disturb him. Ask him to return my call when he has a chance."

The implication was clear: studying, learning, thinking and creating are not important. Those things can be easily postponed. But, a conference—ah, that means that the Rabbi is working for us. Don't interrupt him at his work.

The Rabbi can never be kept so busy that he does not have time to think; so occupied with today that he cannot create for tomorrow; so bogged down with demand and detail that he loses his dreams and visions.

When the Rabbi has time to delve into his books to learn, to formulate new ideas, to develop new programs, to conquer new frontiers of thought and action, to let his imagination run free and to craft the future, then, not only will he be a better human being, feeling better about himself, but the whole community will benefit from the effects of his thinking and his creativity.

Much of the stress and "burn-out" that Rabbis experience will be relieved when the structures in which they work are changed. The proprietary Synagogue will alleviate much of the political tension of the Rabbinate; the life-tenured contract will replace the uncertainty and trauma of contract renewal with security and peace of mind.

But, a good deal of job-related stress is inherent in the Rabbinate. The "Jewish distance" between Rabbi and Congregants means isolation and loneliness. The Rabbi's public persona and time-demanding, erratic schedule mean unusual burdens on spouse and children. The depth of human tragedy and suffering which he shares can mean anxiety and anguish, sadness and distress. No Rabbi leaves a funeral of a young child without his own lingering grief and pain.

So, the Congregation must urge its Rabbi to protect his mental and physical well-being, so that he can continue to serve them in health and wholeness.

No Rabbi can be expected to work seven days a week. No Rabbi can fall prey to the "superman syndrome," assuming that he must teach every class, and that no committee can do without the benefit of his wisdom and vote.

In addition to summer vacations, every Rabbi must take at least one day off during the week. And, every couple of months, he must take off two or three days in a row—preferably out of town, where the telephone won't ring—for refreshment and renewal.

The Synagogue should join with most major corporations in sending its top professional—its Rabbi—for a yearly "executive checkup." Hospitals have developed special physical examinations for business leaders, taking into account their high-stress responsibilities and their sedentary lifestyles. After a thorough work-up, the doctors, then, prescribe the most effective regime of diet and exercise for the busy executive. The Synagogue, no less than any Fortune 500 company, should insist on the best care for its Rabbi.

The Rabbi must make time for proper exercise and physical activity. The Synagogue can help arrange a membership for the Rabbi in the local health club, racquetball court, golf or tennis club. And, the members of the Synagogue must come to understand that the Rabbi means no slight or insult when he refuses the invitation to "eat a little something, Rabbi." There are just so many Bar Mitzvah parties and wedding buffets that any one Rabbi's diet can tolerate.

Finally, the Synagogue must make sure that the comprehensive medical plan it provides for the Rabbi includes payments for mental health counseling and psychotherapy. The Rabbi, like any other human being—and, perhaps, more so—needs a place to talk; an objective listener from whom to seek advice. The psychologist's or psychiatrist's office needs to be available as an option for a Rabbi who wants help. Sometimes, even a Rabbi needs a Rabbi.

Job-related stress and tension will never disappear from the Rabbinate. But, they can be greatly mitigated and lessened by a Congregation which encourages its Rabbi toward mental and physical health and by a Rabbi who learns to take good care of himself.

Once a young man's choice of the Rabbinate as a career was a cause for great joy and pride from his family; respect, bordering on awe, from the Jewish community.

Now, more often than not, the Rabbi hears a question filled with tolerant amusement and sardonic irony: "What kind of job is *that* for a nice Jewish boy?"

But, with new definition, direction and new-found

dignity, the Rabbinate can become, once again, the source of profound professional and personal satisfaction for the men and women who choose this noble calling, and of sacred spiritual and communal leadership for the people they serve.

LEADERSHIP

The new Synagogue will mean new expectations, requirements and commitments for its leaders.

The Synagogue will be enhanced by the consolidation of its programmatic and administrative leadership into one professional—its Rabbi. As every other Jewish organization and every major business—which has a singular chief executive—the Synagogue will now be able to focus on one individual to set its agenda, inspire its ideals and implement its goals.

The new lay leaders will bring deep involvement and new seriousness of purpose to their tasks.

Members of a Synagogue's Board of Directors will be, by definition, personally accountable for their decisions. Their own financial responsibility will mean that the Synagogue will be run in an efficient, business-like, successful manner. With their own reputations and prestige on the line, these Synagogue leaders will always do the best possible job, providing for the needs and the interests of the Jewish community.

These new leaders will take great pride in their work and in their accomplishments. They will see the Synagogue for what it is—the core institution of Jewish life and survival.

Therefore, their commitments of time and energy will be to the Synagogue, not as a stepping-stone to other communal positions, but as a worthy end in itself.

These men and women will return a sense of importance, stature, significance and predominance to Synagogue leadership. Their Synagogue will become, once again, the center of Jewish existence, and they will be honored and emulated for their commitments and their contributions.

To emphasize their positions as Jewish leaders, and to serve as role models for Jewish life and Synagogue membership, Synagogue Board members should take upon themselves serious standards of leadership.

To demonstrate commitment to Jewish observance and values, every Synagogue Board member must attend Synagogue Services regularly, and participate in formal Jewish study throughout the year.

In order to have an understanding of the workings of the Jewish community, and, in recognition of the necessary bond between Federation and Synagogue, every Synagogue Board member must volunteer to serve on the Board of Directors of at least one community agency.

In order to assume the obligation of every Jew to the Jewish and general communities, every Synagogue Board member must be an annual contributor to the local Federation and to the local United Way campaigns.

In order to fulfill the *mitzvah,* incumbent on every Jew, to have a personal connection with the Land and the People of Israel, every Synagogue Board member must have visited Israel, or must participate in his Synagogue's Pilgrimage.

In order to know, firsthand, the principles and the practices of his "wing" of American Judaism, every Synagogue Board member should visit his Movement's Seminary and be an annual contributor to its programs.

In order to keep up with the latest developments in Jewish thought and activity, every Synagogue Board member must be a subscriber to at least two popular Jewish magazines or journals, and read at least four books of Jewish interest each year.

In order to be involved in other phases of Jewish life, and to develop relationships and lines of communication, every Synagogue Board member must belong to at least one other Jewish defense, philanthropic or service organization, such as B'nai Brith, Hadassah or ORT.

In order to keep the Synagogue constantly renewed and vigorous, every Synagogue Board member must be responsible for developing new leadership, by bringing at least one person into Synagogue involvement and potential Board membership.

The top Synagogue leaders must know that their work and dedication will set the example and standard of Synagogue involvement for members of their Congregation.

Yet, at the same time, they must understand that not every member will have the same level of interest or desire for participation.

The sad truth is that the age of volunteerism, as it was once known, is over. The Synagogue cannot expect that unlimited numbers of people will give unlimited numbers of hours to work for it and its programs.

However, many volunteers will be more than willing to come forward for short-term assignments, utilizing their individual talents and abilities. Any project, with a clearly defined goal and a proscribed time span, will attract workers who want personal involvement in Synagogue activities.

Obviously, people with specific, special interests will be most likely to become engaged in projects which reflect those interests: parents of Hebrew School age children may want to create Chanukah parties, Purim Carnivals and springtime picnics. Parents of teen-agers may want to work on dances and weekend retreats. Athletic-minded Congregants may be eager to organize the Men's Club softball team.

While for the most part, the time of cookie-baking volunteers is over, many, many people are still eager to give of themselves to tasks they find worthwhile and fulfilling. People still want to be recognized, needed and appreciated for their unique skills. People still seek ways to share with others, to invest themselves in something beyond themselves, to feel pride and satisfaction at participation and accomplishment.

Synagogue leaders must, therefore, recognize the new kind of volunteerism and provide ample opportunities for giving and doing. The Synagogue programs will greatly benefit from the hours of devoted service, and the volunteers will be happy to have helped.

The Talmud teaches: "As the generation, so the leader; as the leader, so the generation."

Our generation, uncertain and seeking, needs a new kind of Synagogue leader. We need men and women who are deeply committed to the vitality, creativity and survival of the Jewish community. We need men and women who are willing to find the most sensible, successful practices and procedures of the modern world and apply them to the, as yet, uncharted horizons of Synagogue life. We need men and women who will be accountable for their decisions, responsible for their actions and role models for their community. We need men and women who are unafraid to break with the past in order to carve out the vistas of the future.

As this new breed of leader emerges, the Synagogue and the Jewish community can expect tremendous new developments, exciting new dimensions and limitless accomplishments.

It takes but one candle to illuminate the darkness. It will take but a few good men and women—committed, tenacious and accepted—to lead us to renewal and greatness.

MONEY

When it comes to money, the Synagogue—as any other business, and most people—has but two questions to ask: where to get it? And, how to spend it?

Since only 75%–90% of the money which a Synagogue needs to operate will come from membership dues, School fees and donations, the rest of the necessary revenue must come from some form of fund-raising activity.

The problem is that most Synagogues have tried, at one time or another, virtually every fund-raising project known to humankind! Every variation of bazaar, sale, dinner, dance, auction, benefit concert, raffle, casino and bingo game ever conceived has been attempted.

Besides taking a tremendous amount of work by scores of volunteers to arrange, these fund-raising programs have a natural limitation: they will be supported only by a predefined group—the members of the Synagogue and their friends. Helping to meet one particular Synagogue's financial needs has little attraction or appeal to members of the general community.

Sometimes the activities succeed; sometimes they do not. But, no matter how wonderful or lucrative, no project can ever solve all the Synagogue's financial requirements, so, as soon as one activity is over, planning for the next must begin.

Meanwhile, all the other non profit organizations in town are running the same kind of programs to benefit their causes, calling upon many of the same people for attendance and support.

To use an expression popular in the heartland, "You can go to the cow just so often, before there is no more milk left."

The "general rule" of fund-raising is that 80% of the money will come from less than 20% of the people. So, the Synagogue's real task in raising money is to identify the 20% of its population that is capable of making significant contributions and, then, appeal to them in the most productive ways.

Hospitals, Universities, Symphony Orchestras and Theaters have much to teach the Synagogue about fund-raising. These public institutions establish gradations of recognition and reward, in exchange for pre-set levels of gift-giving.

For example: a contributor who gives $25,000 to a particular University becomes a member of the "President's Club," and is invited to have lunch with the President and sit in his private box at a football game. A contributor who gives $10,000 to a Symphony Orchestra joins the "Conductor's Guild," and attends a reception with the guest soloist following an opening performance. All special contributors are listed, according to gift category, in programs, play bills, annual reports and public documents.

These institutions solicit major donations by making their cause appealing and attractive to potential givers. They exude a sense of purpose and importance. They link their institution, and thus, the contributor's name, to consequential ideas and high principles. They offer the incentive of wide public recognition and desirable reward. They, cleverly, let their donors compete with each other to give more, by attaching greater status to larger gifts. They, frankly, appeal to vanity, pride and ego. And, their methods work!

Compare this to the Synagogue's usual attitude: "Give. Give because you should. Give because you have. Give because you must. Give because it's right. Just give."

Like the other non profit institutions, the Synagogue can "market" its fund-raising needs and appeals in the most desirable ways.

Each Synagogue has any number of members who, in addition to yearly dues, (after all, the Symphony's contributors still buy their own performance tickets; University contributors still pay regular tuition for their children) will contribute $1,000, $2,500, $5,000 or $10,000 or more, to be part of a special category of gift givers—if only they are asked properly and recognized sufficiently.

And, there lies one of the great lessons of fund-raising. People rarely give to *causes;* people give to *people.*

Undoubtedly, you receive numerous requests each year for contributions from dozens of worthy organizations. Most appeals come to you in the mail; others come over the telephone. A few are made directly to you, in person, by someone you know.

Unless you are already predisposed to supporting a particular cause, or, unless its mail appeal is super-special, you are likely to throw away most fund-raising letters with the rest of your "junk mail." Unless a telephone call comes at an especially opportune time, you are likely to reject the request.

But, it is different when one of your friends sits down with you, face-to-face, eyeball-to-eyeball, and says, "This cause/institution/organization is important to me. It stands for and accomplishes wonderful things. I've given my own money. I'm here to ask you to support it with me. Won't you consider joining me and giving a gift, too?"

Unless you really don't have the money to give, or unless you have great objection to the cause, or unless you have a heart of stone, you will find it very difficult to turn away your friend. You will, most likely, respond positively and generously to the appeal. And, of course, once you are a committed contributor, you very well may be willing to ask some of *your* friends to join *you* in supporting *your* cause.

It takes a few dedicated men and women, who are willing to support the Synagogue with their own dollars, and who are willing to take the time and expend the effort—and face the risk of rejection and disappointment—to ask their friends to give. One by one, family by family, the Synagogue can build up a cadre of financial supporters, because by demonstrating the Synagogue's importance and worth in their own lives, the solicitors will show potential givers the purpose and the consequence of their gifts. And, when need and personal commitment are established, the response will be positive and generous.

The special contributors should not be expected to be

completely altruistic and selfless in their giving. They, certainly, will get the benefits of inner satisfaction and tax deductions, but, like donors to other public institutions, they deserve more. So, the Synagogue must offer incentive and status, recognition and reward to its contributors.

There are many different ways, besides the usual plaques and nameplates, to recognize and thank special givers, and each Synagogue will find the methods and programs most appropriate for its people. However, the Synagogue must never take its special supporters for granted. Their gifts can mean the difference between financial struggle or fiscal solvency. So, the gratitude of the Synagogue must be publicly, constantly and significantly shown.

Yet, even with all the good that they do, the additional yearly gifts of the special contributors are still not enough to bring the Synagogue long-term financial stability.

No institution, and few people, can live on operating income, alone. In business and personal life, the solution is called "investments." In non profit organizations, such as the Synagogue, the solution is called "endowments."

Through the creation of a series of Endowment Funds, the Synagogue can generate income to help meet its ongoing operating expenses and, at the same time, provide for its long-term financial security.

The Endowment Fund Program works this way:

Contributors give the Synagogue a certain amount of money, which is designated as "principal," and put into a special high interest-bearing bank account (or invested in "blue-chip" stocks and bonds). The principal remains untouched, while, each year, the earned interest is used for a predetermined purpose.

Interest from the Endowment Funds can be used for the general expenses of the Congregation, or for special projects and programs such as: scholarships for the Schools, educational equipment, scholarships for youth activities and summer camps, lectureships and visiting teachers.

The minimum contribution to establish an Endowment Fund will vary from Synagogue to Synagogue, but will usually be about $2,500. Each contributor will name his Endowment Fund (such as: "The Cohen Family Endowment Fund") and be able to honor or memorialize a loved one ("established in memory of their beloved parents, Sam and Sadie").

Specific purpose endowments will require a particular contribution (usually, enough principal so that interest earned, at an average of 10% a year, will provide enough money for the intended use). For example: if Hebrew School tuition is $350 a year, then, an Endowment Fund created to provide a student scholarship for the Hebrew School will take an initial gift of $3,500). Thus, the Endowment Fund can be called, "The Cohen Family Endowment Fund, established in memory of their beloved parents, Sam and Sadie, to provide scholarships for the Hebrew School."

A camp scholarship Endowment Fund will require, for example, $10,000; a Day School scholarship Endowment Fund, $25,000; and an annual lectureship Endowment Fund, $15,000.

Endowment Funds work. One Synagogue established an Endowment Fund Program more than thirty years ago. It began with one family, contributing a few thousand dollars, and, over the years, more and more people have contributed more and more money. Today, the combined Endowment Funds have more than one million dollars in principal.

During the 1950's and '60s, when the Synagogue was filled with young families and hundreds of youngsters, the monies generated from the Endowment Funds provided the "extras" for the Hebrew School and youth programs; scholarships for youngsters to attend summer camp, youth conventions and travel to Israel; the additional equipment and staff necessary to maintain buildings and facilities that were in constant use.

Now the Congregation has grown older; many of the young people have moved away and the neighborhood has changed. The Synagogue still has hundreds of loyal and devoted members, but many are retired and are on fixed incomes. The $100,000 in interest that the Endowment Funds generate each year helps subsidize the Congregation's programs—and its very existence—and means solvency and peace of mind.

The establishment of Endowment Funds demonstrates the Synagogue's fiscal responsibility. Instead of merely responding to the monetary needs of the moment, the Synagogue creates a long-range plan for financial stability. Members of the Congregation, who give the individual Endowment Funds, bespeak the promise that the Synagogue will remain viable and financially healthy, from one generation to the next.

Endowment Funds are gifts of commitment and love. Endowment Funds are the Synagogue's investment in the future.

Many Congregations will establish Capital Funds in order to collect enough money to buy land and build facilities.

Twenty or thirty years ago, the building of Synagogues was a top priority of the Jewish community. The response to Building Fund Campaigns was usually enthusiastic and generous, and Synagogues often met their goals quickly.

Today, land and construction costs have risen dramatically. Most modest Synagogue buildings will cost up to a million dollars to build, and larger, fully-equipped facilities will demand many millions more.

How many communities will be able to raise that kind of money? With all the other desperate needs for Jewish money, how many communities *should* raise that kind of money for bricks and glass?

The age of opulent Jewish edifices must be over. Jewish priorities must be established. If Jewish buildings are to be built, then, they cannot be lavish; they must be functional. Having enough space to conduct all its programs must be far more important to a Synagogue than carved wood and stained glass. The quality of teachers who go into a classroom must matter more than the quality of carpeting that goes on the floor.

One noted observer of American Jewish history puts it all into perspective. He teaches that if we continue to build Synagogues, we should build them on wheels! Then, twenty-five years from now, when the neighborhood changes and all the Jews move away, instead of selling the Synagogue to the Baptist Church, we can just roll it to its next location!

Instead of expending tremendous energy to collect funds for building, and instead of plunging a community into enormous debt, there can be, as described earlier, viable exciting alternatives to having a public Building Fund Campaign. Before any Synagogue decides to raise two, three or six million dollars to build, all alternative means of financing ought to be explored.

But, whatever methods are chosen to raise building funds, every Synagogue must, automatically, increase its fund-raising goal by 30%.

First, no matter how carefully the construction numbers have been figured, and no matter how many contingencies have been put into the bids, very few buildings, if any, are ever finished without exceeding budget. To avoid the heartache and the panic caused by running out of money, the Synagogue must have an extra 10% available for cost overruns.

Next, too many Synagogues build their beautiful new buildings, but forget that, on the day the building opens, costs of utilities, maintenance and insurance will soar. So, every Building Fund should designate 10% of its collection for building maintenance and upkeep. The 10% should, like the Endowment Funds, be put into high yield investments, and the yearly earnings used to help pay the operating costs of the facility.

Finally, building a building should be kept in perspective. A Synagogue is not bricks and rooms, but people and programs. When the Congregation needs to build a building, its sole reason is to have a home for the Synagogue family and its activities. Funding the edifice cannot overshadow or overburden the real purpose of the institution. There must always be enough money for what is really important. The Congregation must, therefore, set aside 10% of its Building Fund collection to help underwrite programs and activities. Interest earned on the invested 10% of the Building Fund will help pay for what goes on inside the Synagogue's new walls.

So, if you are considering building a Synagogue facility, think carefully about your Synagogue's purposes and functions. Build not a monument, but a comfortable home for your Synagogue family. Carefully decide how best to collect the funds you need, and, then, spend your money wisely and well. And, whatever dollars you think you will need, add 30% to your estimate so that you can handle construction contingencies, maintain your facility after it is built and still have enough money left to run the programs and activities that make your new building into a real Shul.

The *real* measure of a Synagogue is how it *spends* its money.

Unfortunately, fixed expenses account for the greatest share of the Synagogue's annual budget. And, the cost of doing business continues to rise at a tremendous rate. Expenditures for utilities, postage, telephone, insurance, worker's compensation and social security co-payments are all escalating. Supplies for the office, the kitchen, the schoolrooms and maintenance grow more and more expensive. Salaries go higher and higher to justly compensate valuable employees and to keep pace with spiraling inflation.

So, the Synagogue is caught in a real crunch. It wants to spend money on programs and activities, but so much is required for operating expenses that there is often little left over. A glance at most Synagogues' budgets will tell the sad story. The greatest percentage of Synagogue income is spent on administration of the facility and operations, while only small amounts remain for ritual, programs, youth activities, adult education and special projects. The real purposes of the Synagogue have become almost unaffordable under the weight of fixed expenses.

But, the Synagogue must be able to fund the activities which define its existence. And, the Synagogue must be able to afford the most qualified, creative staff to run its programs and inspire its people.

To solve this financial dilemma, every Synagogue must have a *People Fund!* When it needs to build a building, the Synagogue has, historically, created a Building Fund. Here, the task is far more important. Instead of building buildings, the Synagogue must build *people.* Instead of building in bricks and glass, the Synagogue builds *Jews.*

Let every Synagogue have a People Fund, with the ultimate goal of collecting no less than one million dollars.

Members and friends of the Congregation will make contributions to the People Fund, and, with the income from the invested monies, the People Fund will send youngsters to camp and Israel; permit needing children to receive quality Jewish education; bring scholars to the Synagogue to teach and inspire; enrich the music program; buy books, journals, records and tapes for the Library; purchase educational equipment for the Schools; underwrite conventions and trips for the youth group; sponsor family retreats; support worthwhile causes in the Jewish and general community and subsidize staff salaries, so that the very best people can be found and hired.

The People Fund can be the source of renewal and creativity for the Synagogue. People Fund monies can be used to experiment with new projects, to pilot new programs, to try the untried. The People Fund permits the Synagogue to have faith in itself, by helping mold its future.

The People Fund parallels the Synagogue's Endowment Funds, but there is a significant difference. The Endowment Funds are established only by certain people who can afford the initial contribution, and each is created to support a specific program or project. The People Fund has no minimum contribution; the monies are used by the Synagogue, as additional income, with no restrictions, and *everyone* participates in the People Fund by giving gifts—this year, next year, every year.

The People Fund is important because it gives the Synagogue the additional income that it needs to function with quality and creativity; because it teaches the vital Jewish lesson that the responsibility for *tzedakah* belongs to everyone; and because it gives the Synagogue true credibility, by defining what a Shul is all about.

The Synagogue's People Fund builds the Jewish future by investing in American Judaism's most vital resources—its people, who will live and teach Judaism's message and values, now, and in the years to come.

Unlike some Christian denominations, which claim that "money is the root of all evil," Judaism teaches that money is a valuable instrument for all the good which it can do.

The Synagogue must use the most effective techniques to raise the money it needs. And, with prudent care and wise choices, the Synagogue must spend its money to best fulfill its sacred purpose—"to glorify God and His Torah."

THEREFORE

More than ever, the Jews of America need the Synagogue to fulfill its three-fold purpose of being a House of Prayer, a House of Study and a House of Gathering and Friendship.

So, with candor and honesty, the Synagogue must see its deficiencies and its mistakes; its failure to touch its people or inspire their lives.

And, then, with a renewed commitment to its guiding

principles, with revolutionary creativity and innovation, relying on both ancient, enduring values and newest technologies and techniques, the Synagogue must transform itself.

With the caring, sharing and determination of us all, it can be done.

Then, the Synagogue's import and influence in our lives will be restored, and it will be, once more, the place that calls each and every one of us to God and His Torah, and hears our resounding, happy reply of Jewish affirmation, participation and love.

Planning Ahead

Even by making sweeping and radical changes, the Synagogue and the Federation will still be far from solving all the problems facing the American Jewish community.

The issues raised here are a litany of the *needs of the moment*—the problems, and their consequences, ravaging Jewish life *today*. The solutions offered are not long-term, permanent answers. They are merely intended to respond to the emergency; to help reverse the trends toward destruction, before it is too late.

No problem which is so complex, and has been so long in the making, can be rectified overnight. So, the American Jewish community must learn productive methods and techniques for grappling with its difficult questions and finding suitable answers.

By studying business and industry, academia and government, we can discover the process that will bring us to recuperation and rejuvenation. Every successful corporation, university and government agency looks beyond the present in order to plan for the future. These institutions do not simply function from day-to-day, but identify and come to grips with the challenges of the years ahead through *long-range planning*.

So, instead of just reacting to the issues of the moment, or being content with "patching-up" a problem here and a crisis there, the American Jewish community must begin the critical and exciting task of seriously planning for its future.

First. Each year, almost every Federated community across the country gives a Young Leadership Award to a

213

man and a woman, under forty years of age, whose commitments and work within the community best embody and exemplify Federation goals.

The "prize" that goes with the Award is an all-expenses paid trip to the General Assembly, the convention, of the Council of Jewish Federations.

This annual General Assembly conducts the business of the Federation by bringing together top leaders and contributors from throughout North America. During the four or five day convention, the 3,000–4,000 delegates participate in conferences and workshops ranging over the full agenda of the Federation's local, national and international concerns and activities. Top leaders from the American government address the Assembly to exhibit support for the Jewish community and Israel. And, Israeli government officials evoke Jewish emotions and inspire Jewish loyalty.

The General Assembly is an exciting and stimulating place to be. But, while there is some special programming for the Young Leadership Award recipients, much of their time is taken up with the hubbub and crush of an in-city, hotel-centered convention—complete with masses of people, receptions, cocktail parties, city tours, and choices of hundreds of one or two hour sessions. There is little opportunity for in-depth study or discussion, for grappling with complex issues, for meeting new people and forming lasting relationships.

So, in order to better reward Young Leadership Award winners; to prepare them for continuing roles in the Jewish community; and to best take advantage of their talents and spirit, the Federation needs to create a new model for leadership training and development.

• Let's establish a *National Jewish Conference Center*.

In a rustic or mountain or seashore location, let's build a retreat/conference center with comfortable, well appointed rooms, first rate service, excellent food and full recreational facilities.

Instead of—or, perhaps, in addition to—attending the

Federation's General Assembly, the annual Young Leadership Award winners will come to the Conference Center for a full week, to a program called the National Young Leadership Kallah (Retreat).

There, away from the pressures and responsibilities of business and family, and unaffected by the glitter of a large convention, these young leaders can meet and learn.

With long, concentrated hours available, classes and seminars can be held on a variety of topics. There should be classes on Jewish history, with specific emphasis on the American Jewish experience; on Jewish law, customs, ceremonies, traditions and celebrations; on Jewish thought, theology and philosophy; on the concept of community, *tzedakah* and Jewish responsibility; on the denominations of American Judaism; on Christianity and Islam; on the formation of the American Jewish community and its social service agencies; on the history of Zionism and modern Israel; on Israeli geography, historical sites, government and politics; on communication and group skills; on program development and fundraising techniques; on budgeting and allocations.

Because of the lovely setting and the prestige attached to the Kallah, the most effective and inspirational teachers in the Jewish world will be glad to volunteer their services as instructors. So, the participants will be exposed to the best minds and the most creative practitioners in the Jewish community, who will challenge them to learn and think.

All week, the participants will eat together and meet at the pool, the tennis courts and on the hiking trails. The Kallah will continue over Shabbat, so there can be *davening,* singing and celebrating.

During these seven days, some 400 of American Jewry's most able and talented emerging young leaders will get to know each other, share information about background, family, hometowns, and learn about and from each other. New friendships will be made and new relationships formed.

When the participants leave the Kallah, they will have

learned and studied, for a full week, about their history and destiny, their Jewish inheritance and responsibility. And, they will be part of a network of knowledgeable, committed friends and associates who will fan out across the country to bring new ideas and new inspiration to their home communities. The relationships forged during that one week will mean that the next generation of Jewish communal leaders, from across North America, will know each other and be able to call on and work with each other throughout a lifetime of Jewish service.

Three years after their attendance at the National Young Leadership Kallah, each year's participants should be invited to return to the Conference Center for Alumni Week.

During Alumni Week, advanced classes will be offered and in-depth seminars conducted. Three years' work for the Jewish community will be evaluated, friendships renewed and commitments deepened.

Alumni Week will permit former Kallah participants to meet the newest young leaders; to serve as role models for them; and to extend the country-wide Jewish network even further.

If the National Young Leadership Kallah is a good, productive, useful program, then, it will be even better "the second time around."

In the National Young Leadership Kallah, some may see reflections of the United Jewish Appeal's Young Leadership Cabinet—a fine program, already in place, in the Jewish community.

The Kallah is not meant, in any way, to compete with the Cabinet, but to benefit from its successes.

By definition, the UJA's Young Leadership Cabinet is limited to a select group of people. The Kallah will broaden the base of emerging Jewish leadership to include large numbers of people—representatives from every Jewish community in North America.

Working together, the Young Leadership Cabinet and

the National Young Leadership Kallah can shape the quality of Jewish participation and leadership in this country for decades to come.

The National Jewish Conference Center will not be used by Federation groups, alone. Other organizations and institutions, which want informed, inspired leaders, will take advantage of the Center, too. For example:

Each of the national Synagogue groups can bring its leaders to the Center for classes, seminars and experiences similar to what is offered at the Federation's Kallah. No less than the Federation, the Synagogue needs competent, knowledgeable, caring leaders, and the Conference Center can provide the training they need.

Rabbis from the various "wings" of American Judaism can come to the Conference Center to meet and talk. Instead of taking "pot-shots" at each other from the pulpit and in the press, Rabbis will find that there is much on which they can agree, and, when they must disagree, they can do so in friendship and with respect. American Judaism can ill afford the divisive enmity which so often separates the denominations and their leaders. The Conference Center can well be the place where the arguments can be contained and the healing begin.

The Conference Center can bring together Jews, Christians and Moslems to learn about each other's faith and practices; to discuss sensitive political issues; to know each other on a personal basis. And, the Conference Center can be the place where the Jewish and Black communities begin to talk again, to reforge their once strong alliance.

The beginning of world peace and the end to religious and political strife will *not* come from out of the National Jewish Conference Center. But, when people of different backgrounds, colors, faiths and beliefs meet and talk, the world *is* one step closer toward understanding.

The future of the American Jewish community will be shaped, first, through *people*. A National Jewish Conference Center will be the place where *people* come to learn, to be inspired and to form the friendships and working relationships which will sustain the newly revitalized Jewish community in the decades ahead.

• Next. The American Jewish community needs a *"Think Tank,"* where information is exchanged, trends analyzed, needs identified, ideas formulated and the future shaped and molded.

Most academic and government Think Tanks fall into the trap of hiring a permanent staff of people, whose only job is "to think." Well paid, sitting in their comfortable offices, these thinkers are far away from the day-to-day "nitty-gritty" realities of their subjects. Wrapped in the aura of the status attached to intellectual debate, they are, sometimes, lulled into believing that theory is practice, that ideas can stand wholly independent of experience.

The thinkers of the Jewish community are not immune from making the same kind of mistakes. They forget, for example, that the most brilliant Hebrew School curriculum, designed by the greatest Jewish educators, breaks down in the face of the real-life vagaries of carpools, "snow days" and Little League practice.

What the American Jewish community needs is a Think Tank which is pragmatic and ever-evolving.

It must be a Think Tank which has input from every segment of the Jewish community—religious and secular; professional and lay; organized and unaffiliated. It must listen and respond to the incredibly diverse opinions and needs within the Jewish community. It must be aware of current realities; bold and daring enough to accept, reject and take risks.

The Jewish Think Tank must ask the hard questions and find worthy, satisfying answers: What do we want Jewish life in America to be? What are our needs, our hopes? How will people be, once again, "turned on" to the beauty of Jewish lifestyle and values? How do we make

our worship more appealing? our learning more intensive? our involvement more energetic? How do we develop the programs that will speak to the hearts and
minds of our children, our teen-agers, our young mar-
rieds, our singles, our families, our seniors, ourselves?
How do we ease tensions between organizations? eliminate waste and duplication? make our institutions more
effective? How do we balance our love for America and our
passion for Israel? How do we best share Israel's mission
and help her achieve it? How do we raise the money we
need? How do we spend it, once we have it? Do we care if
our grandchildren are Jewish? how do we best make sure
that they will be? Who will lead us? who will speak for us?
who will inspire us? How do we bring excitement, passion, commitment back to Jewish life? What do we want
our American Jewish community to be five years from
now? ten years from now? into the 21st century? What
are our Jewish goals, and how do we best meet them?

Simply, and profoundly, the Jewish Think Tank must
devise long-range plans and strategies for the creative
survival of Jewish life in America.

The Jewish Think Tank will be inter-disciplinary.
Carpool driving mothers have as much to teach about the
design of Hebrew Schools as do Jewish educators. Business executives know as much about management and
office administration as any Synagogue Executive Director. Stockbrokers, accountants and bankers are profi-
cient with finances, budgets, investments and spending.
Architects, interior designers and contractors bring experience in building and construction. Teachers know educational theory; advertising and public relations people
know marketing and publicity. Computer program designers, artists, librarians, musicians, attorneys, radio
and television personalities, speech pathologists, real estate developers, physicians, bus drivers, chefs, store owners, printers and bakers—anyone and everyone—can
apply his or her knowledge and expertise to solving the
problems of Jewish life in America.

The Jewish Think Tank will be mobile. Most American Jews live in the "Boston-Washington corridor," and most of this country's Jewish "action" is there. But, there are Jews in Idaho and West Virginia; in big cities and small towns; in large Congregations and tiny Shuls. Different Jewish settings mean different Jewish successes and failures, problems and needs. So, the Jewish Think Tank must see, hear and know everyone, everywhere; because from out of Georgia or Arizona, just as well as New York or New Jersey, may come an idea that sparks Jewish renewal.

The Jewish Think Tank will be multi-dimensional, independent and unafraid. The Think Tank will begin with the premise: everything that is wrong with Jewish life in America *can* be fixed. But, to be effective, the Think Tank must be willing to tackle any issue, any topic, any problem. There can be no "sacred cows," no off-limit subjects, no protected turf or personalities which are immune from discussion or debate.

There is, of course, no magic formula, no one answer, which will solve the array of inter-connected problems facing American Jewry. There is no one plan that can be formulated which will guarantee a vibrant, creative future. And, given the autonomous, decentralized structure of the American Jewish community, there is no way to demand that any Think Tank finding be accepted; no way to enforce compliance with any suggestion or recommendation.

But, the Jewish Think Tank *will* be the place for new ideas to be born. The problems of the American Jewish community will be identified and analyzed with stark, raw honesty. The best thinking, from a multitude of sources—ancient and modern—will be applied. New approaches, innovative models and revolutionary plans will be developed.

One by one, issue by issue, problem by problem, the Jewish Think Tank will confront the afflictions that are eating away at the very fiber of the American Jewish community and, methodically, resolutely and assuredly, turn potential self-destruction into dynamic renewal.

The future of the American Jewish community will be shaped, through *ideas*. A Jewish Think Tank will be the place where the best minds of the American Jewish community plan for the Jewish future by grappling with problems, developing new *ideas* and formulating new strategies. From out of the Jewish Think Tank will come the creativity, imagination and innovation which will sustain the newly revitalized Jewish community in the decades ahead.

• Finally. Where does a young Jewish scholar turn for help with his research? Where does a Jewish educator get support for a new project? How does a Federation or a Synagogue find funding for a pilot program? Who encourages a Jewish writer, composer or artist to keep at his solitary task? How do new ideas get translated into Jewish action and experience?

To encourage and support creative expression, the United States Government has, for decades, sponsored the National Endowment for the Humanities, which gives financial grants to promising individuals and groups. From grant recipients have come the academic research, the fiction, poetry, drama, art and music which have helped define America's cultural soul.

The Jewish community needs the equivalent of a National Endowment for the Humanities—which we can call the *National Jewish Endowment Foundation*—to support the creativity of resourceful and inventive men and women, whose talents will give shape to the future of Jewish life in America.

The National Jewish Endowment Foundation should have at its disposal at least one million dollars each year to distribute in grants. Individuals and organizations will submit proposals for projects, and each project will be evaluated on the basis of its inherent merit and its poten-

tial for contribution to Jewish life. Grants of up to
$25,000 will be awarded, so *at least forty* new, imagina-
tive project ideas and experiments will be funded each
year.

Proposals will come from every segment of the Jewish
community, including Federations, Synagogues, Schools,
universities, Rabbis, educators, academicians, authors,
composers, artists and playwrights. In addition, people
who can use their own professional skills to develop
programs that will benefit the Jewish community will
seek support. So, grant proposals will come from computer programmers, business executives, marketing and
advertising people—anyone and everyone who wants to
use his knowledge and talents to improve the quality of
Jewish life.

As with any other expenditure of venture capital,
scholarship monies or prospectus underwriting, some
projects will fail; some will have limited benefit. But, "out
there," somewhere, are the two or six or sixteen ideas
which, when translated into reality, will help rejuvenate
the Jewish community and have the potential to change
the face of Jewish life in America.

Some of the most dangerous and exasperating words
in the Jewish vocabulary are, "but, we've *always* done it
that way." The "seed money" provided by the National
Endowment Foundation will permit the Jewish community to break out of the molds of safe, cautious repetition
and, instead, to reach for new, as yet, unexplored vistas of
innovation, creativity and achievement.

The future of the American Jewish community will be
shaped through *creativity*. The National Jewish Endowment Foundation will enable Jewish thinkers and doers to
have the resources to dream the dreams, take the risks,
try the untried, create the projects and develop the programs which will sustain the newly revitalized Jewish
community in the decades ahead.

- At certain times every year, there will be a convergence of the National Jewish Conference Center, the Jewish Think Tank and the National Jewish Endowment Foundation.

The National Jewish Conference Center will set aside a number of its rooms and workshops for the recipients of the Endowment Foundation grants to be "in residence" for a week or two or a month or two. Sometimes, a creator needs a quiet, secluded place to think and do, and the Conference Center can be just that place.

When a number of grant recipients are in residence at the Conference Center at the same time, they will be able to discuss their projects with each other, exchange ideas, "brain-storm," and sharpen their thinking. It is very probable that, with so many creative people together in the same place at the same time, the outcome of their individual work will be better than it might have been, because each will benefit from interacting with all the others, and the sum of the work will be greater than the individual parts.

The grant recipients will come to report on their work-in-progress to meetings of the Jewish Think Tank. For, as the Jewish Think Tank grapples with the questions of Jewish directions and survival, the creative projects coming from the National Jewish Endowment Foundation fellows will provide answers and vision for long-range planning.

Finally, the National Jewish Endowment Foundation grant recipients will meet with the people of the Young Leadership Kallah, so that the functional and creative elements of the Jewish community can get to know each other, interact and build networks of friendship and cooperation for shaping and assuring the Jewish future.

- The National Jewish Conference Center, the Jewish Think Tank and the National Jewish Endowment Foundation will take significant amounts of money to create and sustain. From where will that money come?

First. Across Jewish America, some $650–$700 million is raised by Federations each year. Approximately $350–$400 million of that total goes to Israel; the rest is kept in the local communities.

To fund the institutions that will forge the Jewish future in America, let's set up a very simple five year plan.

For the next five years, before making any allocation either to Israel or to a local agency, let every Federation contribute 1% of its collected dollars to the *Fund for the Jewish Future*. That means that, each year, some $6½–$7 million will be put in the Fund. In five years, the Fund will have $35–$40 million in principal, including accumulated interest.

Invested with a yield of 9%–10%, the Fund of the Jewish Future will generate $3½ million or more each year.

Three and one-half million dollars is not enough to do everything that must be done by the National Jewish Conference Center, the Jewish Think Tank and the National Jewish Endowment Foundation, but it is a significant beginning.

Second. To raise the bulk of the needed money, the American Jewish community must provide for itself what, over the past few years, it has been providing for Israel.

In 1979, then Israeli Prime Minister Menachem Begin called upon the Jewish world to join in partnership with Israel to fund what became known as Project Renewal.

Begin's plan was to generate enough money to raise the standard of living for a large segment of Israel's population. A very real economic gap existed (and, sadly, continues to exist) between the Ashkenazi and the Sephardic communities, and between long-time Israeli residents and newly arrived immigrants. With an infusion of new money into Israel, Begin reasoned that educational services could be upgraded, cultural programming enhanced, and housing and community centers rehabilitated and built anew.

To facilitate fund-raising, and to make the needs more intimately felt, more than a score of American Jewish communities "adopted" towns and villages in Israel. The American contributors could visit their "twin" cities, meet the residents, and feel a personal connection with the people to whom they were giving.

Since 1979, the American Jewish community has raised more than *$165 million* for Project Renewal!

Those dollars are being put to good and worthy use, and they must continue to come, so that Israel can grow and develop.

But, our own strength, our own future, our own survival is at least as important as Israel's. If Israel needs $165 million for renewal, then, so do we! It is time for a *Project Renewal for the American Jewish community!*

The contributions that come to *our* Project Renewal will not detract from the giving to Israel, because when need is demonstrated, generous, committed people will continue to give what they must.

So, let's set, for helping *ourselves*, the same goal that we set for helping Israel. Over the next five years, in addition to each Federation's annual 1% contribution, let's raise $165 million for the Fund for the Jewish Future!

Then, we will have enough money to properly fund the National Jewish Conference Center, the Jewish Think Tank and the National Jewish Endowment Foundation.

• Many of the concepts presented here have already begun to take shape—not in theory, but in reality—through the brilliant and visionary work of one of the most respected and creative Jewish leaders of our time, Rabbi Irving (Yitz) Greenberg.

Rabbi Greenberg has created an organization which he calls CLAL, in the spirit of Clal Yisrael, the unity of the Jewish People.

CLAL wants to prepare and motivate Jewish leaders; to help people and institutions understand the newly unfolding age in Jewish history; to upgrade the resources of both people and ideas in the Jewish world.

To achieve its goals, CLAL has: its programming and educational division, *Shamor,* which brings charismatic, talented teachers to instruct top lay leaders, to present programs and publications for Jewish education and renewal; *Am Echad,* to promote inter-movement understanding and interaction, to bring together Rabbis and lay leaders for dialogue and discussion promoting unity and increasing cooperation between segments of the Jewish community; *Zachor,* as a Holocaust Resource Center, to commemorate and explore the Holocaust as the starting point of a new era in Jewish history; and *Beit CLAL,* a retreat center for study and leadership training.

So, the ideas offered here are not just academic theory; they are not unrealistic or unattainable dreams. Rabbi Irving Greenberg, through CLAL, has already started the process of planning for and creating the Jewish future.

Some of the proposals here complement what Rabbi Greenberg has already done. Some go far beyond his program. CLAL may prove to be the instrumentality through which many of these ideas can be focused, or CLAL may serve as the model for newly emerging vehicles of Jewish renewal.

CLAL's experience and success serve as the foundation and the inspiration for continuing efforts to move the Jewish community toward growth and change. For CLAL, and the National Jewish Conference Center, the Jewish Think Tank and the National Jewish Endowment Foundation, funded by the Fund for the Jewish Future, all proposed here—and other projects and programs that will be developed along the way—will help forge and assure the creative survival of Jewish life in America.

• The American Jewish community must begin, now, to plan for its future. We cannot be without direction; we cannot leave our growth and development to whim or chance; we cannot simply be "reactors" on the stage of history.

The choices we make now, the leaders we teach and train, the ideas we formulate and the projects and programs we create, will all have a tremendous impact on how the Jewish future will be shaped. We must know what we want, we must plan how to get there, and, then, we must take decisive, positive action to achieve our goals.

The advertising slogan is right. "Tomorrow begins today."

What Now?

Jonah, the reluctant prophet, came to tell the people of Nineveh that, through their own misdeeds and mistakes, they were about to destroy themselves and their city.

Instead of reacting to Jonah's words with anger or arrogance—or, simply ignoring him—the people of Nineveh looked around and saw what their folly had wrought. Immediately, they began to repent and change their ways, before it was too late.

And, the people of Nineveh saved themselves and their city from destruction.

To look at Jewish life in America today is to see the result of apathy and indifference; the lack of participation and the lack of commitment of the past two decades.

Yet, all is far from lost.

For, well aware of the ultimate consequences, and, truly desiring to improve Jewish life—for themselves and for others—a number of individuals and organizations have, in recent years, carved out new ways to make Jewish life intellectually stimulating, spiritually uplifting and personally fulfilling.

• For example: In 1960, the Jewish Theological Seminary created the Melton Research Center for Jewish Education.

Funded by a very generous gift from Samuel Melton, of Columbus, Ohio, the Melton Center develops and publishes curriculum for afternoon Hebrew Schools and provides teacher training, professional conferences and consultations with Schools.

The Melton Program has resulted in new, exciting ideas about afternoon Jewish education, and has crafted some outstanding curriculum.

But, *after twenty-five years*, the Melton Center has still not produced an entire, unified five-year Hebrew School curriculum.

Another example: In 1969, at the General Assembly of the Council of Jewish Federations, held in Boston, the proceedings were picketed by a group of young Jewish activists. They called upon Federations to spend more energy and money on Jewish education, to improve the quality of Jewish life in North America.

To respond, in part, to this passionate demand, in 1972, the Council of Jewish Federations founded the Institute for Jewish Life.

The Institute's mandate was to review and evaluate the qualitative aspects of Jewish life, make recommendations for reform and, then, solicit and fund ideas and projects to bring about swift and significant improvement and change.

Funded by contributions from individual local Federations, and headed by two distinguished Jewish educators—first, Dr. Leon Jick of Brandeis University, and later Rabbi Kenneth Roseman of Hebrew Union College—the Institute began to identify and grapple with problems and develop creative solutions.

But, the impact of the Institute never had a chance to be felt. In 1976, the Institute for Jewish Life went out of existence.

The Institute had found it very hard to have its critical evaluations and recommendations for change accepted by the very same institutions that were funding it.

As worthy and as successful as the Melton Center and the Institute for Jewish Life—and the many other organizations like them—have been, they suffer from a fatal flaw which plagues all large, formally constituted institutions.

Bogged down either by the necessity of reaching a

widely acceptable consensus, or circumscribed by the need to protect narrow self-interests, *institutions* often move too slowly and ponderously to accomplish much, or to have any real effect on immediate needs.

A few attempts at influencing the quality of Jewish life have been made through the *personal* vision, determination and money of *single* individuals.

A prime example is the Kohl Center for Learning in suburban Chicago.

In the early 1970's, Dolores Kohl—a woman with a dream and enough money to fulfill it—created the Jewish Teachers Center. The Center's intent was to provide educational tools and materials, teacher training and support, and classroom approaches and methodologies for teachers in Jewish schools.

Because of its success, the Kohl Center now has branches in Jerusalem and Beer Sheva, and has expanded its horizons to include secular learning and a Children's Museum. This concept of a teacher learning/resource center has spawned more than forty Jewish Educational Resource Centers throughout North America, where teachers can find materials and strategies to make their instruction creative and exciting.

Further: The concern and passion of two distinguished teachers have produced periodicals which have significantly affected Jewish thought and debate over the past dozen years.

Rabbi Eugene Borowitz, of New York, publishes *Shma: A Journal of Jewish Responsibility*, a bi-weekly which has already produced more than 300 issues, discussing the great Jewish concerns of our time.

Leonard Fein, of Boston, founded *Moment*, a monthly magazine, which has much popular appeal and a widening circle of loyal subscribers. *Moment* recently celebrated the publication of its 100th issue.

The Kohl Center for Learning, *Shma, Moment*—and the many other Jewish projects like them—prove that *one individual can* make an important contribution to Jewish life by identifying a need, embracing a cause and pursuing a dream.

What remains to be seen is if these kinds of projects will have a life of their own—beyond the personal commitment, determination and money of their creators. If they do, then, their impact will ripple into the next generation. If not, then, at least, Jewish life, in our time and place, has been greatly enhanced by these precious gifts of caring and love.

• Two innovative responses to the problems of Jewish life in America—one concerned with Jewish learning; the other, with Jewish living—have had such a major impact that they have already become an integral part of the American Jewish landscape.

First: In 1976, the first "Conference on Alternatives in Jewish Education" was held at Brown University in Providence, Rhode Island.

Sponsored by a committee, originally convened by the North American Jewish Students' Network, the Conference drew 350 participants. People involved in Jewish education, from across the entire spectrum of Jewish experience—professional and lay; teachers and students; religious and secular—shared educational ideas, strategies, philosophies, methodologies, failures and successes.

From the first Conference, came a second, where the Coalition for Alternatives in Jewish Education (CAJE) was born.

Now, the annual CAJE Conference attracts more than 2,000 dedicated, positive, innovative people, who come from across North America, to teach, study and learn from and with each other. They meet and talk; they share ideas, learn new techniques, examine new books and materials, and find out that they are not alone in their quest to bring excitement and creativity into Jewish schools.

Then, inspired by their experiences, infused with a new spirit and rededicated to their tasks, they return to their home communities to implement what they have learned with their own students, and to share their new-found knowledge with other teachers.

During the year—between Conferences—CAJE publishes a newsletter and maintains a computer listing of members with special talents and interests, who are willing to share their skills with others. In many communities, "Mini-CAJE Conferences" are held, so that teachers, everywhere, can benefit from workshops and study sessions.

Supported by gifts and grants from individuals and a few local Boards of Jewish Education and Federations, CAJE, nevertheless, still scrounges for operating monies, because few national Jewish organizations are yet willing to fund this "maverick" coalition.

But the lesson ought to be very clear. When the "establishment" institutions did not adequately respond to the needs of their people, then, individual Jews did what needed to be done *for themselves, by themselves*.

Through the vision and determination of a very few people—with very little money, with almost no institutional support—the Coalition for Alternatives in Jewish Education has become one of the most powerful, dominant and positive forces for Jewish education in North America. Its impact has been felt in virtually every Jewish classroom, and its energy will continue to influence the direction of Jewish education for years to come.

• Perhaps the single most effective and far-reaching contribution to the quality and vibrancy of Jewish life, during the last twenty years, has been the formation of the Chavurah.

Chavurat Shalom, the prototype of the modern Chavurah, was established in Somerville, Massachusetts, in the fall of 1968.

Born to be an alternative to traditional Jewish institutions, Chavurat Shalom was founded by several young Rabbis, graduate and undergraduate students attending colleges and universities in the Boston area.

In the midst of the turbulent '60's, these were Jews who were seeking meaningful ways to deepen their Jewish knowledge and to participate in an ever-evolving Jewish lifestyle. Many were "alumni" of Camps Ramah, USY and LTF, who were no longer comfortable with the formality of the Synagogues of their youth, or with the authoritarian atmosphere of most institutions of higher Jewish learning.

Drawn together by their mutual search, they created, first, what was to be a Seminary for the training of Rabbis for a new generation. Though that part of the experiment was never fulfilled, the men and women of Chavurat Shalom *davened* together, celebrated Shabbat and Holidays with each other, and studied and learned from one another. A few of the members lived in the Chavurat Shalom house, committed to *kashrut* and Shabbat observance.

Soon, a similar group of young Jews formed the New York Chavurah. Friends and acquaintances of Chavurat Shalom members, the New Yorkers followed the Somerville model of a community devoted to Jewish learning and observance. Though there never was a communal living arrangement, New York Chavurah members studied, prayed and celebrated together.

From these two early models came dozens of individual, independent Chavurot. Springing up on college campuses from coast to coast, these Chavurot often took the form of a Bayit (House) where young Jews connected with each other to explore Judaism and grow in mind and spirit. Rather than join a fraternity or sorority—complete with Greek alphabets, hazing and secret handshakes—

young Jews of the late '60's and the early '70's began a
return to their own heritage, by bringing new forms to
ancient teachings.

Moving from college campuses to urban settings, in
the mid 1970's and into the early '80's, the Chavurah has
become the focal point for Jews who want to express their
Judaism, without the need for formal structures or insti-
tutionalized settings.

Guided by the principles of independence, self-
determination, democracy and egalitarianism, capable of
leading their own *davening*, planning their own celebrations and learning Torah from and with each other,
members of most Chavurot have little need for a Rabbi or
professional Educator; little tolerance for the politics or
the fund-raising bazaars of the contemporary Synagogue.
They find their satisfaction in their prayers, their learning
and the extended family they create with each other.

The Chavurah idea has spread throughout the coun-
try. The New York Chavurah evolved into the West Side
Minyan, and, then, into the Minyan Ma'at. Other notable
Chavurah-like groups formed: the Fabrangen in Washing-
ton, D.C.; the Germantown Minyan and the B'nai Or
Fellowship, both in Philadelphia; the Library Minyan in
Los Angeles.

Today at the Anshei Chesed Synagogue, on Manhat-
tan's Upper West Side—a Synagogue facility that, thirty
years ago, had more than 1,000 member-families, and,
five years ago, could barely find a *minyan* of ten—there
are six different Minyanim going on, at the same time,
every Shabbat. Along with the renaissance of New York's
Upper West Side, has come a rebirth of Jewish life. But,
rather than seek out established Synagogues in order to
express and live their Judaism, the new West Side Jews
have chosen to form their own Chavurot and Minyanim,
as their way to God and Torah.

Over the years, some Synagogues have been farsighted enough to invite independent Minyanim to meet

in their basements, libraries, chapels and classrooms. Other Chavurot still alternate between living rooms, or rent small facilities. But, wherever they are, Chavurot mean vitality and vibrancy for Jewish life, because a few Jews still care enough about their Judaism to "do it themselves."

From the independent Chavurah was born the Synagogue-based Chavurah, developed by Rabbi Harold Schulweis, of Encino, California, and discussed earlier.

The Synagogue-based Chavurah differs from the independent Chavurah in that its members, first, choose to join a Synagogue, presumably, for its professionally led Services, its Hebrew School and its full program of activities. Only later, do they seek out a smaller community within the community, for intimacy, friendship and fellowship.

But, the Synagogue-based Chavurah ultimately succeeds for the very same reasons that the independent Chavurah succeeds: a small group of people band together, in mutual commitment and friendship, in order to explore and experience Jewish living and learning with each other.

Now, there are so many people involved in both independent and Synagogue-based Chavurot, that, a few years ago, a National Chavurah Conference was called to bring Chavurah members together to share experiences and learn from each other. The annual Conference attracts hundreds of caring, "turned on," satisfied Jews to days of prayer, study and inspiration.

The Chavurah has, literally, transformed Jewish life in America. In less than twenty years, the Chavurah has grown from a handful of seekers, living outside Boston, into a massive movement of thousands of groups of sharing and fellowship, in every city and town in America.

Searching for Jewish answers, wrapped in Jewish commitment, involved in Jewish ritual and learning, and devoted to each other, Chavurah members teach us all what it means to be Jewish.

Thus, the Chavurah proves, once again, that when the institutions of Jewish life do not adequately respond to the needs of their people, individual Jews can and will be Jewish *for themselves, by themselves*.

The inherent danger in successful innovations—such as CAJE and the Chavurah—is that, over the years, the innovators may become as settled in and as cautious as the establishment which they sought to change.

But, to an American Jewish community, which is currently in search of its soul, the creative innovators teach us the emerging truth: unless we are willing to be the generation that nonchalantly and silently witnesses the demise of a 3,800 year old religious heritage—which has been given to us as a precious gift—then we must take immediate, positive steps to rejuvenate and revitalize Jewish life.

In order to have a dynamic, personally and communally fulfilling Judaism, we must move the established institutions—the Synagogue and the Federation—to understand and respond to our needs. Or, we must strike out, on our own, to create the forms which will satisfy and sustain us in the years ahead.

How do we do it?

In 1974, *Judaism*, a quarterly journal, published by the American Jewish Congress, conducted a Symposium entitled, "Where Do I Stand Now?"

Twenty-six scholars, writers, religious leaders and academicians responded to a series of questions designed to take stock of attitudes towards American Jewish life and the outlook for its future.

One of the Symposium participants was William Novak, then a young writer and editor of the independent Jewish review, *Response*. Novak has gone on to become the co-editor of *The Big Book of Jewish Humor*, the author of *The Great American Man Shortage*, and most recently, the co-author (read: "ghost-writer") of the best selling autobiography, *Iacocca*.

Responding to the question, "What is your outlook on religion in general, and Judaism in particular? Novak wrote:

"As we begin to imagine the limits of technology, it becomes increasingly clear that the basic questions of our lives are still unanswered. These last few years have seen a return to religion, and this trend will continue, although the *old religious forms may be bypassed. I now see a new Judaism being developed*, one which is peculiarly American, and which derives directly out of the Chavurot communities and similar sensibilities in the Jewish counter-culture. *This new Judaic impulse is fed by the best qualities in each of the recognized branches of Judaism: the authenticity of Orthodoxy, the liberalism of Reform, the scholarship of Conservative Judaism, the social awareness of Reconstructionism, (and) the excitement of Chassidism*. In addition, we must add to this recipe the ingredients derived from recent Jewish history: the effects of the Jewish experience in Israel, Europe, the Soviet Union and America during these last fifty years. This new Judaism is not a movement, but a decentralized series of shared concerns and values. . . ."

It can be done.

Judaism can grow, develop and evolve to meet the challenges of a new place and a new time.

Chaim Potok teaches us that *we can* create a new era of Jewish life, and William Novak begins to teach us how.

There are many suggestions in this book for blending the best of Judaism with the best that contemporary America and the modern technological world have to offer.

The rest of what it takes to shape and mold the Jewish future is *in you*.

What can you—as an individual—do to enrich your own Jewish life and, by extension, the Jewish life of your family and your faith community?

You can change the Synagogue and the Federation. You can create the Jewish institutions that you want. You can formulate Jewish life *for yourself, by yourself*.

All it takes is desire. All it takes is your decision to make Judaism a meaningful, consequential part of your life. All it takes is your commitment to enrich your life through God and Torah.

Dennis Prager, the internationally acclaimed writer and lecturer, radio talk-show host and co-author of the popular book, *The Nine Questions People Ask About Judaism*, teaches that Jewish "labels" are worthless.

It does not matter if you call yourself Orthodox, Conservative, Reconstructionist or Reform. It makes no difference if you describe yourself as religious or secular, a "good" Jew or a "bad" Jew.

There is only one designation that really counts. Are you a *serious* Jew?

If you are a *serious* Jew, then, you will want to be wrapped in the ethical mandate of Judaism; you will want to rhythm your existence to Judaism's life-enhancing rituals. You will respond to the call of Torah and hear the voice of God summoning you to greatness.

You will want to assure the viable, creative survival of Judaism. And, you will know that it can be done.

But, if your answer to the question, "Are you a *serious* Jew?" is not a positive, affirming, "Yes!" then, your answer cannot be a simple, disengaged, "No." For, your answer must reflect your potential and your ability to grow.

"Are you a *serious* Jew?"

"No, not *yet*." "Not yet. But, I am ready to explore

and discover the beauty and the worth of my religious heritage, to seek God and find Him, learn Torah and live it, embrace the members of my faith community and love them.''

What now?

It's up to you!

It's Up To You

Elie Wiesel, the conscience of a nation, the storyteller of our generation, remembers this:

In the barracks of Auschwitz—in the filthy, dehumanizing, degrading conditions of the death camp—it came time for Simchat Torah, the rejoicing over finishing the yearly cycle of the Reading of the Law.

One old man went from one fellow prisoner to another:

"Tonight is Simchat Torah. Tonight, we must dance and sing and celebrate."

"Crazy old man," they said. "We have nothing to celebrate; there is no reason to rejoice. Look at us. We are like animals: no clothing, no food; freezing, being worked to death; the stench of the ovens filling our nostrils. And, besides, even if we wanted to observe Simchat Torah, we have no Torah. How can we dance with the Torah, when we have no Torah?"

The old man paused for a moment, and, then, walked over to a little boy—five or six years old.

"Tell me, son," he said. "Do you know how to say the *Shma Yisrael?*"

The little boy seemed puzzled, but, he looked up at the old man and said:

"Of course. Of course I know how to say the *Shma*."

"Say it for me," demanded the old man.

"Here? Now?" asked the boy.

"Here! Now!" insisted the man.

The little boy stood up, a bit hesitant and confused, but, loudly and firmly, he said:

"*Shma Yisrael, Adonai Elohanu, Adonai Echad.*"

"Hear, O Israel, the Lord is our God; the Lord is One."

"You see," cried the old man. "We *do* have a Torah. This little boy is our Torah. Torah is in him."

And, the man picked up the little boy, and held him high over his head, and began to dance and sing.

And, very soon, every prisoner in that bleak, filthy concentration camp was dancing and singing, and celebrating Simchat Torah.

And, they all danced until dawn.

Torah is in you. Torah is in me. Torah is each and every one of us.

In *you*, in your heart and in your hands, in your mind and in your soul, is all the faith, all the love, all the justice, all the compassion, all the human dignity that Torah teaches.

Torah is within *you*. You have the power and the ability within you to sanctify time, to turn ordinary moments into holy happenings.

And, *you* have the power and the ability within you to make the secular and the mundane into the spiritual and the sacred.

You have the power and the ability within you to hear eternal truths and enduring values, to embrace justice and right.

And, *you* have the power and the ability within you to touch another's soul with your compassion and your love.

You have the power and the ability within you to *be* Torah and to *live* Torah—to assure Jewish survival and renewal by the choices you make, by the way you act.

To claim that the *future of Judaism* depends on you, and how you live your Torah, means so overwhelming a responsibility, so onerous a burden, that it is far easier to ignore the challenge than to confront it.

But the reality is far more stark, more frightening, more challenging, more exciting and, ultimately, far more satisfying.

Your own future,
your own life,
your own identity,
your own humanity,
your own values,
your own emotional health,
your own personal relationships,
your own most intimate quests, needs and hopes,
depend on the kind of choices that you make—starting
now!

And, then, the choices you make for yourself will help
shape and forge the future of the whole Jewish People.

For, I learned from Arthur Kurzweil, the chronicler of
Jewish genealogy, and the author of *From Generation to
Generation,* that going back only ten generations, each
one of us has 1,024 direct ancestors.

Each decision, each word, each action of every one of
those 1,024 people helped determine who and what *you*
would be.

If any of those people had lived in a different place,
received a different education, prepared for a different
career, married a different person, gotten in the way of a
different pogrom, had different commitments, made different choices, then, everything—everything—would
have changed.

Each choice *you* make—this day and every day—
affects you, your spouse, your children, your parents,
your community—and the 1,024 people who will be the
ten generations of *your* descendants.

Look at Jewish life in America today. You can help
preside over its demise, permitting the covenant of the
ages to end in you. Or, you can assure your own well-
being and happiness, your responsibility to the past, and
your answer to the future, by working toward renewal, by
carving out new directions for Jewish life for yourself and
those around you.

How do you do it? How do you assure the Jewish
future for yourself and your children's children?

Listen to the Torah within you. Celebrate, laugh, cry, give, share. Always reach for the best. Don't settle for mediocrity; don't let pettiness and politics separate you from enduring truths and eternal values. Love yourself, love each other, love God and live His Torah. Act, everyday, as if the future of Judaism, and the future of the very world, depends on you alone. It does.

Be heartened by the words of the ancient Prophet, Jeremiah:

> "Restrain your voice from weeping and your eyes from tears, for you shall be rewarded . . . There *is* hope for your future . . ."

And, be inspired by the words of Theodor Herzl, the prophetic advocate of the modern State of Israel:

> "If you really, really want it, it is no dream."

And, finally, be energized by the summons of the modern genius entertainer-philosopher, Walt Disney:

> "Tomorrow's world approaches. Let us explore, question and understand. Let us go forth and discover the wisdom to guide (us) through the uncharted seas of the future. Let us dare to fulfill our destiny."

Live your Torah with courage and with joy. Let Jewish renewal and new directions for Jewish life come *from within* you, *because of* you and *through* you.

Dare to hope. Sustain the dream. Never give up. Keep the faith.

The best is yet to be!

Glossary

(H) Hebrew

(Y) Yiddish

Aleph-Bet (H)

The first two letters of the Hebrew alphabet; denoting the entire Hebrew alphabet, as "ABC's" denotes the entire English alphabet.

Aliyah (H)

literally: to go up; to go up to live permanently in Israel; also, to go up to the platform in the Synagogue where the Torah is read and to recite the blessings over its reading.

Amcha (H)

literally: Your people; meaning, God's people, the Jewish people.

Ashkenazi (H & Y)

literally: German; denoting Jews who are descended from Germany, Central and Eastern Europe.

Bar/Bat Mitzvah (H)

literally: son/daughter of the commandment; a Jewish child, on reaching the age of 13 (12½ for a girl), who then becomes obligated to observe the commandments of Torah; also the public Synagogue ceremony, where the young man/woman first exercises the privileges and responsibilities of fulfilling the commandments, usually by having an *aliyah*, reciting the blessings over the Reading of the Torah.

245

Bayit (H)	literally: house; name for a communal living arrangement, where, usually, Jewish Holidays and dietary laws are observed by the residents.
BCE (English)	Before the Common Era; historical time period before the year 0; commonly known as BC.
Bet Din (H)	Rabbinic Court; usually consisting of three Rabbi-scholars, who decide on questions of Jewish law and controversies between Jews, and preside over Jewish divorces and conversions to Judaism.
Bimah (H)	platform, higher than floor level in the rest of the room, from where Jewish worship is conducted and the Torah is read.
Bracha (pl: *ot/as*) (H & Y)	blessing; prayer of thanks/praise to God, beginning with the formula, "Blessed/Praised are You, O Lord our God . . ."
Bris/Brit (Y & H)	literally: covenant; the ritual circumcision of male Jewish children on the eighth day of life; the physical sign of the spiritual covenant between God and the Jewish People.
Bubbie (Y)	Grandmother.
CE (English)	Common Era; historical time period after the year 0; commonly known as AD.
Challah (H)	braided egg/white bread, usually eaten on the Sabbath and Jewish Holidays.
Chanukah (H)	literally: dedication; the Festival of Lights, celebrating the victory of

the Maccabees over the Syrian oppressors in 168 BCE and the re-dedication of the Holy Temple in Jerusalem; observed in the winter, usually in December.

Chavurah (pl: *ot*) (H)   friendship groups of people who band together to study and celebrate Jewish life; an extended family.

Chevra Kadesha (H)   literally: holy friendship group; the Holy Burial Society; Jews who perform the task of preparing and burying the deceased.

Cheder (Y)   literally: room; a Jewish school, taken from the "one-room schoolhouse;" implying an old-fashioned place and atmosphere of learning.

Chumash (H)   literally: five; one of the Hebrew names for the Torah—the Five Books of Moses.

Daven (Y)   to pray; to worship God either individually or as part of a group; implying being caught up and involved in the experience and emotions of prayer.

Drash (H)   literally: explanation; an explication and interpretation of a weekly Torah Portion.

D'var Torah (H)   literally: a word of Torah; a homily/"mini-sermon" on a weekly Torah Portion, usually drawing a moral/ethical lesson from the text.

Haftorah (H)   a lesson from the Biblical Prophets, chosen, by the Sages, for its thematic relationship to a particular Torah Portion; chanted following the Torah Reading every Shabbat and Holiday morning.

Ha Motzi (H)	literally: the bringing forth; name of a blessing/prayer recited before eating bread/food; "Blessed/Praised are You, O Lord, our God, who brings forth bread from the earth."
Halacha (H)	literally: the path/way; Jewish Law; implying "the way to go/the path to walk on."
Hashgacha (H)	Rabbinic supervision and authorization of meat/food, to assure that the Jewish dietary laws are being observed.
Kaddish (H)	a doxology; a prayer praising God; found in every Jewish worship Service; in one of its forms, known as the "Mourner's Kaddish," it is the prayer recited by mourners for eleven months following the death of a close relative and, then, each year on the anniversary of the death.
Kallah (H)	retreat; usually religious and spiritual in nature.
Karpas (H)	green vegetable used as part of the Passover Seder ritual to symbolize springtime.
Kashrut (H)	Jewish dietary laws.
Kehilah (H)	Jewish community; implying a community organized to take care of its own communal/social responsibility needs.
Kepa (H)	head-covering; skullcap; worn by Orthodox Jewish men at all times; by other Jewish men (and, in modern times, some women) at prayer, study and while eating to show respect and reverence for God.

Kinder (Y)	children.
Kibbutz (pl: *im*) (H)	collective farm/living arrangement in Israel based on the socialist principle of shared work and shared reward.
K'lal Yisrael (H)	the totality of the Jewish People, united in purpose and action.
Kohen (H)	priest; in Biblical times, the officiant at the Temple rituals; now, a descendant of the Priestly Tribe, who has certain privileges and responsibilities in regard to Jewish ritual; implied is the role of pastor.
Maftir (H)	the last section of a weekly Torah Portion; sometimes implies Haftorah, because the person who recites the blessings over the reading of the last section most often chants the Haftorah.
Mara d' Atra (Aramaic)	literally: master of the land; local Rabbinic authority; each Rabbi who has jurisdiction in his own Congregation/community.
Maror (H)	bitter herbs; the bitter herb/vegetable used as part of the Passover Seder ritual to symbolize the bitterness of Egyptian slavery.
Menshlikite (Y)	the attribute of being a human being who is humane, kind, decent, compassionate.
Mikvah (H)	literally: collection; ritual pool of collected natural waters, used for ritual purification; immersion is done by: a bride before her wedding; a married woman following her monthly menstrual flow; a prospective convert as a ritual of con-

version; a scribe before writing a sacred text; some Jewish men before the Sabbath

Minyan (pl: *im*) (H)   literally: the quorum of ten people necessary for conducting a public Jewish worship Service; also, any Jewish religious Service; also, a group of people who have banded together to worship and study.

Mitzvah (pl: *ot*) (H)   literally: commandment; a ritual or ethical command/mandate of God; common usage: "a good deed."

Mitzvah Chevra (H)   a friendship group dedicated to doing a specific command/good deed.

Navi (H)   Prophet; implied is social conscience.

Nechemta (H)   comfort/consolation.

Oneg Shabbat (H)   literally: joy of the Sabbath; a social gathering held on the Sabbath to celebrate the Sabbath, either at home with family and friends, or in the Synagogue following the Service.

Pareve (Y)   neither meat nor dairy; a neutral category of foods, according to Jewish dietary laws; food which can be eaten with either meat or dairy.

Pesach (H)   the Festival of Passover, celebrating the redemption of the Jewish People from Egyptian slavery; observed in the early spring, usually in April.

Rachmonos (Y)   compassion.

Rashi   Rabbi Solomon ben Isaac; 11th century commentator on the Bible and

	the Talmud; his commentary is often referred to as "the Rashi."
Rav (H)	Rabbi; implies authority, specifically in regard to the matters of Jewish law.
Rebbe (Y)	Rabbi; implies charismatic leadership.
Schvitz (Y)	steam-bath.
Seder (H)	literally: order; the ritual meal, held on the first two nights of Passover in remembrance and celebration of the Exodus.
Sedra (H)	a weekly Torah Portion.
Sephardic (H & Y)	literally: Spanish; denoting Jews who are descended from Spain, Mediterranean and Middle-Eastern countries.
Shabbat/Shabbas (H & Y)	literally: Sabbath; the Jewish Sabbath, which occurs each week from sundown on Friday to sundown on Saturday; a time of prayer, family celebration, physical rest and spiritual rejuvenation.
Shaddchan (H & Y)	marriage match-maker.
Shavuot (H)	literally: weeks; the Jewish Festival commemorating the giving of the Torah at Mt. Sinai; observed seven weeks after Passover, giving it the name, "weeks;" observed in late spring, usually May or June.
Shidduch (H & Y)	marriage match.
Shiva (H)	literally: seven; the seven day period of intense mourning, following the death of a close relative.
Shtetl (Y)	small town/village; usually implies close-knit Jewish community of Eastern Europe.

Shtiebel (Y)	tiny Synagogue; implies small, close-knit Congregation in a limited geographical area, such as a *shtetl* or in a particular neighborhood; implies Orthodox ritual and piety.
Shuk (Arabic & H)	market-place; usually open air; in Israel, today, most notably the Arab market in East Jerusalem.
Shul (Y)	literally: school; now, Synagogue; so named because often, particularly in Eastern Europe, the functions of Jewish worship and learning would take place in a one-room building.
Simcha (H & Y)	a joyous occasion; *bris, Bar/Bat Mitzvah,* wedding, happy celebration.
Simchat Torah (H)	literally: rejoicing of the Torah (Law); Jewish Holiday when the yearly Torah Reading cycle is completed and, immediately, begun again; a time of joyous celebration; observed at the conclusion of the Festival of *Succot,* usually in late September or early October.
Succot (H)	literally: booths/tabernacles; the Jewish Festival commemorating the ancient harvest and the continually renewing process of nature; observed in the early fall, usually in late September or early October.
Tallit(s) (H)	prayershawl; worn by male Jews (and, in modern times, some females) at morning prayer; shawl-like garment, with fringes on its four corners, knotted to be a symbolic reminder of the 613 commandments found in the Torah.

Talmud (H)	code of Jewish law, written between the 3rd and 7th centuries CE; an enormous compendium of law, legends and homilies; still the basis for Orthodox practice and Jewish legal decisions.
Tefilot (H)	prayers.
Tephillin (H)	phylacteries; leather boxes, attached to arm and head with leather straps, containing parchments with sections of Torah; worn by Jewish males (and, in modern times, some females) during weekday morning prayer.
Tochacha (H)	warning/admonition.
Torah (H)	The Five Books of Moses; also the handwritten parchment Scroll, containing the Five Books of Moses.
Treif (H)	literally: torn; non-kosher food.
Trup (Y)	musical cantillation by which the *Torah* and *Haftorah* portions are chanted; the symbols, called accents or notes, which represent the musical cantillation.
Tush (Y)	colloquialism: rear-end, backside, posterior.
Tzedakah (H)	literally: righteousness; usually simply and incorrectly translated as "charity;" implies the obligation of human beings to share their bounty with each other.
Yeshiva (H & Y)	a school of higher Jewish learning; a Rabbinical Seminary.
Yiddishkite (Y)	Jewishness.
Yom Kippur (H)	Day of Atonement; observed ten days following the Jewish New Year

in late September or early October;
a twenty-four hour period of prayer,
repentance and fasting.

Yontif (Y)   Yiddishized version of the Hebrew
                                 Yom Tov; literally: Good Day; A
                                 Jewish Festival/Holiday.

Zayde (Y)   Grandfather.

Temple Israel

Minneapolis, Minnesota

IN MEMORY OF
CLARA SKOU
FROM
GEORGIA & IVAN KALMAN